LITTLE FOXES that spoil the vines

LITTLE FOXES

that spoil the vines

W. B. J. MARTIN

ABINGDON PRESS

NASHVILLE AND NEW YORK

LITTLE FOXES THAT SPOIL THE VINES

Copyright © 1968 by Abingdon Press

Standard Book Number: 687-22150-1

Library of Congress Catalog Card Number: 68-17448

Scripture quotations unless otherwise noted are from
the Revised Standard Version of the Bible, copy-
righted 1946 and 1952 by the Division of Christian
Education, National Council of Churches, and are
used by permission.

The chapter entitled "Restlessness" was published
previously as "The Resting Place of Life" in *The
Expository Times,* Jan., 1965, Vol. LXVVI, and is
used here by permission.

The extract from the poem "Ducks," in *Ducks and
Other Poems* by F. W. Harvey, is reprinted by permission of the author's representatives and of the
publishers Sidgwick & Jackson Ltd.

SET UP, PRINTED, AND BOUND BY THE
PARTHENON PRESS, AT NASHVILLE,
TENNESSEE, UNITED STATES OF AMERICA

preface

Catch us the foxes,
the little foxes,
that spoil the vineyards.

—SONG OF SOLOMON 2:15

When William Temple, later Archbishop of Canterbury, was an undergraduate at Oxford, he went to hear a famous American evangelist who pressed upon his student congregation the forgiveness of God, quoting the text, "Though your sins be as scarlet, they shall be as white as snow." Temple said, "Though I went to the meeting in a serious, enquiring spirit, I found myself quite unmoved, for, alas, my sins were not scarlet, they were gray—all gray. They were not dramatic acts of rebellion and violent self-affirmation, but the colorless, tired sins of omission, inertia, and timidity."

As Solomon knew, it is the "little foxes" that spoil

the vines. Despite the hymn, not many of us are "guilty, daring souls." What spoils life for us is often some small and silly habit, some almost trifling stupidity. To put it in Tennyson's words,

> It is the little rift within the lute,
> That by and by will make the music mute,
> And ever widening slowly silence all.

But preachers often ignore these small spoilers; they prefer to deal with some large abstraction called "sin," and so become guilty of answering questions nobody is asking and dealing with problems remote from everyday experience.

When one lives close to a congregation, one discovers that people are not so much vicious as vain, not so much tough as touchy. "Evil is wrought by want of thought more than by want of heart." Like Thomas Carlyle, many a man can rise to a great occasion who collapses under a straw. That tetchy genius surmounted the loss of manuscript, thrown into the fire by a careless maidservant, and without a word of complaint immediately set to work to rewrite it from scratch. This was the same man who was put into a rage by the crowing of a cock in a neighbor's garden, and made his wife's life miserable by his peevish complaints over trifles.

As a parish minister, I rarely encounter downright wickedness. I am not often called in to deal with cases of dramatic crime or vice. What I meet with is stupidity and silliness, like a husband resenting his wife taking a job—and making a success of it! Like a wife's uncontrollable urge to spark life up by creating a scene. Much domestic unhappiness is caused by lack of communication between man and wife, by the inability or unwillingness of one partner to take the trouble to articulate himself. A lot of personal failure is due to some small flaw, like a trigger-quick reaction to what threatens security or disturbs routine.

These are all small things in themselves. I recognize, of course, that they may root back in big things, like a fundamentally faulty attitude to success and failure, to rights and privileges, to dependence and independence. They are symptoms of a deeper malaise. But many of them are capable of rectification on their own level and, indeed, unless rectified, will exacerbate and inflame the conditions out of which they spring. I am of the opinion of Stanley Jones, when he says, "It is easier to act yourself into a new way of thinking than to think yourself into a new way of acting." By paying attention to the small habits and gestures of daily life, one may cultivate an attitude of reverence, of sensitivity, and of courtesy that can affect the whole personality.

Our failure to do this is often a mark of pride. That homespun philosopher, Josh Billings, once said, "A woman will sometimes confess her sins, but I never knew one to confess her faults!" If it is true, she shares this reluctance with men. It does not hurt our self-esteem to unite with a congregation in a general confession. Indeed we may almost feel smug about acknowledging that we "have erred and strayed from thy ways like lost sheep" and that we are "miserable sinners"; but let any man become specific about our known faults, such as irritability, unpunctuality, or rhetorical exaggeration, and we are immediately on the defensive.

So, though I realize that there are great and desperate sins calling out for treatment from the pulpit (and in other places have done my little bit to call attention to them), I make no apology for finding a place and a time to deal with the "little foxes that spoil the vines."

contents

failing to mind your own business

They made me keeper of the vineyards;
but, my own vineyard I have not kept!

—SONG OF SOLOMON 1:6

The very man who coined the phrase "little foxes" was convicted of the fact that he had allowed one of the commonest and most destructive of those little foxes to slip into his own garden.

There he was—a busy man, entrusted with public and civic responsibilities which he discharged with great success, administering a kingdom with brilliant efficiency. Yet when he surveyed his own private garden, he found it overrun, neglected, despoiled. "Alas," he cried; "they made me keeper of the vineyards; but, my own vineyard I have not kept!"

That is such a human failing—the failure to mind one's own business—that we see evidences of it all around us. Like Solomon, many a man is wiser for others than he is for himself. Indeed, the temptation to neglect one's own patch seems to be fairly common among wise men, among intellectuals and members of the learned professions.

Is it not part of our folklore that ministers' children often come to a bad end? Actually it is folklore and not fact. In fact, this country owes more than it is sometimes aware to sons and daughters of the manse. How many big business men, executives, writers, actors, journalists, and teachers stem from the parsonage! How many career diplomats and public servants are children or grandchildren of missionaries! Why, when I look out upon my own modest congregation, I can count at least five "preachers' kids," all of them active in civic and church affairs.

But there is just enough truth in the old saying to make it stick. Fathers who devote the bulk of their time to counseling others—preachers, psychiatrists, physicians—are often so emotionally spent when they reach home that they have only the fag ends and butts of themselves to give to those who are nearest and dearest to them.

This is not altogether untrue of many busy business-men. A man who expends endless thought in planning and running a large business organization may show no imagination or finesse at all in securing the harmony and liveliness of his family circle. He knows that in a large firm, people must be treated as human beings—encouraged, recognized, humored—otherwise he is going to lose the best of them. But at home? I often think that many a top executive would lose his secretary in a month if he treated her in the same casual way as he treats his wife. And many a salesman who has the Dale Carnegie course at his fingertips when dealing with clients and colleagues fails to realize that his closest colleagues are his own children. But in that vineyard he is often so unintentionally careless as to be brutal.

There is a verse in Proverbs which says, "The eyes of a fool are on the ends of the earth." I never read that verse without thinking of the character in Dickens' *Bleak House* named Mrs. Jellaby. When she wasn't helping the missionaries by sewing red flannel petticoats for the dusky maidens of the South Seas, she was endlessly engaged in writing letters to reform this and that. She was the busiest woman in England. But her own home was a pigsty, and her own children were the biggest little savages in the street. She could see everything at a distance of two thousand miles, but to what was immediately under her feet she was totally blind.

Many of us are like that. We mind everybody's business except our own. We evidently concur with Mark Twain that "to do right is wonderful. To teach others to do right is even more wonderful—and much easier!"

But in writing this chapter about minding your own business, I am aware that I am treading on very dangerous ground. Many people need no such advice; they are already doing that—and nothing else. Like the lady I met the other day who told me virtuously, "I try to be a Christian; I keep myself to myself." Such people need no encouragement from me. They need to be reminded that Christianity does not mean being respectably aloof, but becoming richly involved.

The real Christian is the original tightrope walker. His life is lived precariously balanced between minding his own business and minding other people's business. For he realizes that he cannot do the one without the other. Is not this the point of Christ's famous saying, so often misunderstood, that a man ought to love his neighbor as himself? Some outgoing, activist Christians try to behave as though Jesus had said, "You must love your neighbor better than yourself," or even, "You shall love your neighbor and hate yourself."

But in fact that is impossible. A man who hates himself is incapable of loving others. As a Christian educator once said, "You cannot teach children to love others out of insecurity and fear. Only the child who is loved is capable of loving others. Only the child who respects himself can show respect to others." And the same is true of adults. Show me the man who is full of bile and spleen toward others, who hates his fellowmen, and I will show you a man who hates himself.

This is the reason, and the only reason, why a man

should love himself: that he might be capable of loving others. For no man who does not respect himself, and find himself fun to be with, is going to enjoy other people.

So let's look at the state of our own vineyards! Some years ago Christopher Morley wrote a book with the lovely title, *The Man Who Made Friends with Himself*. Shouldn't we begin there? For the blunt truth is that many of us are our own worst enemies. To put it in Christina Rossetti's words:

> Myself, arch traitor to myself,
> My hollowest friend, my deadliest foe,
> My clog whatever way I go.

When I look back over my own life, I discover that I have done more harm to myself than any man has ever done to me. Or is ever likely to do to me.

Well then, how does a man make friends with himself? First of all, he does it by being realistic about himself. I am certainly no friend to myself if I habitually pull the wool over my own eyes. Yet a lot of us do just that. We flatter ourselves that we are easygoing, when in fact we are just plain lazy; we like to characterize ourselves as people with strong convictions, when in fact we are simply pigheaded and stubborn. We maintain that we are terribly busy, when all the world knows that we are just undisciplined in the use of our time.

In New York, where all things are possible, there used to be an office where, for a small fee, one could go for a criticism session. With complete objectivity the staff would put the client wise about his slovenly posture, his slurred speech, his ungainly walk, the style of his hair and the cut of his clothes. I believe they did quite a business; but, of course, it was all on a superficial level. One of the main values of public worship is that week by week—and for an equally modest fee!—one may be exposed to much more radical and searching criticism. Who can attend a church regularly without being compelled to listen to home-truths that the natural man in us is anxious to avoid? If a man will open his life to inspection by the living God in Jesus Christ, he will be left in no doubt as to his real self. The words of Jesus will sear his soul. Paul's hymn of love will reveal the shallowness of what he has come to accept as a standard of relationship.

The other ingredient in the recipe for making friends with yourself is the humble decision to let *God* punish you—if that is what he wants to do.

So many people are spoiling life by trying to punish themselves. And very often they are the least religious people among us. Eric Hoffer, the longshoreman-philosopher of California, says that when modern man throws aside his belief in a Savior, he is compelled to spend twenty-four hours a day trying to be his own savior. When he discards his belief in the atonement, he tries to make his own atonement. But even those who believe theoretically in the atoning work of Christ are often guilty of this. They never make the glad discovery that forgiveness is a fact; that God is far more anxious to restore us than to punish us, far more anxious to renew us in grace than to keep us groveling in subjection. It was said of Nietzsche that he took Jacob's words at Peniel, "I will not let thee go, except thou bless me," and twisted them into "I will not let thee go, except thou curse me." When one watches some people at their religious exercises, one gets the same impression. They do indeed "wrestle with God," but not to their enlargement and enlightenment. They seem bent on hearing not the good news of liberation, but the bad news of deprivation and diminution. They use religion to restrain and inhibit; they seem to value it for the threat it holds over them.

If a man is to keep the little foxes out of his vineyard, he has to learn to let the Lord of the vineyard do the pruning and the sifting. And this he will assuredly and sure-handedly do, since he knows what to preserve and what to destroy. The Man who made friends with himself and with all the world knew this well. "I am the true vine, and my Father is the vinedresser. Every branch of mine that bears no fruit, he takes away, and every branch that does bear fruit he prunes, that it may bear more fruit."

careless listening

Take heed then how you hear.

—LUKE 8:18

Of all the "little foxes that spoil the vines" I am inclined to think that the most pernicious and insidious is careless listening, especially in family relations, where people spoil life for one another by their inability to listen to what is being said.

I have to confess I am not an expert on the subject of good listening. What preacher is? A preacher has been defined as a man who would cross a continent to deliver a sermon, but would not cross the street to hear one. That is a libel, but it has just enough truth in it to make it sting. On the whole, public orators are better talkers than they are listeners. So let me shelter behind a text, this word of Jesus recorded by Luke: "Take heed then how you hear."

Isn't that an extraordinary thing to say? Not "take heed *what* you hear," but "take heed *how* you hear." We are not altogether responsible for what we hear, but we are responsible for how we hear it, for the degree of attention we give to it, for the manner in which we receive it, and for the length of time we hold it in mind.

Many people fail to realize that there is an art of listening. Listening can be cultivated or neglected. It can fall into various categories. There are such things as sloppy listening, close listening, creative listening, listening with the third ear (to quote the title of Theodor Reik's book). Alas, some of us do not employ two ears in listening, much less a third! And there are other types— intermittent listening, selective listening, greedy listening, to enumerate but a few. And is there not deliberate non-listening? Consciously and unconsciously, we all spend an enormous amount of energy shutting out sounds we do not wish to hear. As W. H. Auden has pointed out, in any modern city a great deal of our energy has to be expended in *not* seeing, *not* hearing, *not* smelling. "An inhabitant of New York who possessed the sensory acuteness of an African bushman would very soon go mad."

Seeing that the subject is so complicated, let me single out three types of listening for special attention.

The most common and harmful type of listening is what might be called egotistic listening. Some of us pay close attention only when we ourselves are the object of the conversation. While our neighbor is relating that boring story of how he climbed the Matterhorn or got chased by a bear, we are merely waiting for him to finish so that we can butt in with our account, such a pretty story, of how we were blessed by the pope at St. Peter's.

I happen to be one of six children. When I was a boy my mother used to embarrass us kids by going off once a month or so to visit a fortune-teller. We were ashamed that she was so simple and naïve, or perhaps we feared that she might get to hear from the seer's lips some things about ourselves that we preferred to keep secret! In any case, there came a time when we began to be more sympathetic; we realized what was happening. Once a month, on her visit to Madame Claire Voyant, seated in a darkened room, dear Mum was the absolute center of attention. After dealing with six children, each of whom imagined he was the sole object of concern and consideration, she found it was quite a change to have a listening ear all to herself. And all for fifty cents! Today, maybe she would be off to the psychiatrist, paying him twenty-five dollars an hour, but the idea would be the same. But I must say this for Mother: for the other thirty days of the month, she was the best listener there ever was; she was completely and selflessly absorbed in the triumphs and failures, the questions and problems of her brood.

Naturally, she did not have to cultivate this: she loved

us. But most of us lesser mortals do have to cultivate it. Being so naturally egotistic, we have to watch ourselves constantly lest we give an ear only to what concerns us and us alone.

Another inferior form of listening is selective listening, the refusal to pay attention to what we do not want to hear, or to screen out what is unfamiliar and disturbing and controversial. Francis Bacon, who, when he wasn't writing the plays of Shakespeare, produced some pretty good essays, once said, "Read, not to confute and contradict, but to consider and learn." He had in mind that numerous class of people who only read to support what they already believe or to rebut what they do not agree with. But that is not reading to listen; that is reading merely to rearrange one's prejudices.

Does a hawk ever listen to a dove? Do conventional Episcopalians ever listen to Bishop Pike and Malcolm Boyd? Do Democrats ever listen to Republicans? It is, or used to be, an American conviction that truth was arrived at through the clash of dissent. What the mind repudiates at first hearing may turn out on closer examination to have some validity to it. If it is not swallowed hook, line, and sinker, it may help to modify, to improve, to enrich our present understanding. Unorthodox opinions, such as that the world is round, that disease is carried by germs, that Englishmen have no sense of humor, have all been stoutly resisted at one time or another. But fortunately there have always been a few listeners willing to set aside their prejudices and to attend long enough to hear what was being said.

Unhappily, they are far outnumbered by the selective listeners. Like the young man who said to me once, all unconscious of his arrogance, "I don't believe in a life after death. The idea of going on forever and ever doesn't appeal to me; it leaves me cold." That's egotism for you! To put one's feelings and personal preferences in place of ideas, convictions, rational judgments. To say of anything, "I like it" or "I don't like it" is not an argument; it's a mental hiccup. This young fellow dismissed a belief that has held the ages in thrall because it did not "appeal" to him. With one lordly gesture he swept aside the intellectual arguments of philosophers from Plato to Alfred North Whitehead. On the basis of personal preference, he cocked a snook at the instinct that built the pyramids, that sent Christian martyrs to their deaths with amazing courage, that brought into being not only some of the finest Christian art but also the sacred books of the East—and let us not forget that reincarnation and the transmigration of souls is not the fad of a few old ladies in California, but the settled and rational faith of nearly half the world. To dismiss all this on the flimsy evidence of one's "feelings" is arrogance indeed. It entails an unwillingness to listen, not only to some of the world's most creative thinkers, but to the stifled voices of the bereaved and to the clarion voice of

Jesus, whose love of life and mastery of it makes him immortality's chief spokesman.

A third form of inferior listening is intermittent listening. There was a story that appeared in the *New Yorker* some time ago which concerned a man, an average man I reckon him, who was given to the nasty masculine habit of attending to female conversation with only half an ear. After a hard day in the office he returned home one evening, settled in the armchair to read the paper, and dimly heard his wife chatting away about the events of her day. After a while he thought, "Well, I'd better pay some attention to what she is saying." And when he tuned in, it was to hear her say that the man next door had made a pass at her. He was so indignant that he would have gone out there and then and horsewhipped the dog. "When did this take place?" he inquired. "It didn't take place," was the reply. "I've simply been telling you about a dream I had last night."

Intermittent listening can lead one into a lot of trouble!

The only form of listening worthy of a man is what I would like to call creative listening. All real listening is creative listening. It is far more than just letting sounds bang on the eardrum; it is cooperating with those sounds. One recalls here the response of the listeners to the prayer of Jesus in Jerusalem before the Feast of the

Passover. As Jesus prayed, "Now is my soul troubled. And what shall I say, 'Father, save me from this hour'? No, for this purpose I have come to this hour. Father, glorify thy name." John records that he was answered by a voice from heaven. But of those who stood by, some said it was thunder; some said, "An angel has spoken to him."

To some people all that breaks upon the ear is "thunder," a natural phenomenon, nothing more, nothing but. Life is nothing but the struggle for existence, music is nothing but the scraping of horsehair against catgut, honesty is nothing but the best policy, the voices that spoke to Joan of Arc were nothing but her imagination. But other people hear behind the cry of the poor the still, sad music of humanity; they hear behind the thunder the voice of God; and behind the tumult and confusion of human history they hear the divine voice calling them to closer cooperation and commitment.

And these same people hear not only the divine voice, but also the human voice. The story is told of an old missionary in Africa who had labored single-handed in a lonely mission station for many years. Finally the society scraped up enough money to send him a colleague. The young man arrived fresh from seminary, with honors thick upon him. The chiefs and natives assembled to bid him welcome, and finally the young fellow was called upon to respond (in English, because he had not yet mastered the dialect). Somewhat pompously he began, "We must always remember that there is the Eternal

Gospel, and the temporary manifestation of it." The old missionary stood up at his side to translate this, "Friends," he cried, "he says he is very glad to see everybody." That was real listening and real interpretation. The older man was listening, not merely to what his colleague said, but also to what he meant to say and what he surely would have said had he been more sure of himself!

I often wish that when I was a young minister, fresh from school, more intent on afflicting the comfortable than on comforting the afflicted, there had been such a wise old interpreter at my side saying, "Friends, he says he loves everybody." For that was what I was really trying to say in my funny, awkward way.

If we all tried to learn the art of creative listening, what we could do to interpret people correctly to one another, for some of us are bent on doing ourselves an injustice! If we listened—really listened—to the voices of our children, to their unspoken questions and their unuttered cries for help, how blessed would be our homes.

boredom

Not long ago a young man, hardly more than a boy, was arrested for killing three perfect strangers. The only explanation he could offer for this senseless, tragic act was, "I was bored." Boredom is indeed a killer. One does not have to be a depth-psychologist to realize that it is precisely boredom that lies behind much of the vandalism, reckless destruction, and wanton aggressiveness that mars not only the ghettos, but the smooth, shiny surface of suburban America. Even among the young, one finds a *tedium vitae* that makes them unwilling or unable to cope with the sheer amount of time and energy they find on their hands. They set out to "kill time"—what a horrible and revealing phrase!

But boredom is not confined to juvenile delinquents. Nor does it always assume physical expression. Many a respectable matron indulges in careless talk to ease her boredom. Gossip, which is one of the nastiest little foxes in the human zoo, is often an attempt to jazz life up by exaggeration and innuendo, or to give zip to a dull party. And life gets so dull for some married couples that from time to time they feel the urge to manufacture a crisis. They deliberately provoke a scene just to see the sparks fly and to break up the drab routine of life.

But the really serious thing about boredom, to my mind, is that its hosts of victims do not even recognize what is "bugging" them. They are not consciously aware of the disease that is spoiling their lives. Because this is so, I think it important to try to analyze and uncover the ailment and to distinguish different types of it. Let it be said that they are not all of equal importance, nor are they all necessarily bad. In fact, some are not bad at all. A peasant in the Middle Ages could accept a lot of boredom, routine, and sameness that would drive us silly, simply because we have been brainwashed into thinking that all life must be entertaining, continuously exciting; must, as we say, be "fun," and above all must contribute to our happiness. I like the reply of the headmaster of the famous Choate School, who, approached by a parent who expressed the hope that her son would be happy there, said, "Madame, we are not in the happiness business!" Perhaps it would be better if more schoolmasters had the courage to say that.

Looking at the phenomenon of boredom, there are, it seems to me, five types.

First, what might be called the common or garden variety of boredom, the irreducible element of routine and monotony in every task. No amount of dancing about in the kitchen is going to make the washing of diapers, the cleaning of greasy dishes, tidying up, anything other than chores. Reading aloud to one's children, however much one loves them, is bound to be a fatiguing business for an intelligent parent. The vapid adventures of Jane and Dick are a sorry substitute for *Herzog* or *The Wall Street Journal*. And it is well to bear in mind that there is no job, however glamorous it looks on the surface, that does not contain huge chunks of boredom. Think of the hours that actors spend hanging around on the set, that concert pianists spend keeping their fingers supple, that authors spend correcting proofs, that trial lawyers spend assembling evidence. There is no profession that is exempt from hours, even days, of sheer humdrum routine.

But there is a second type of boredom, which might be dignified with the name "calculated boredom," like spending an hour on a bridge watching the water flow by. To me one of the most boring jobs in the world seems to be that of the mailman, trudging along with a bag on his shoulder. Yet I have done precisely that, with great joy and without any payment. I called it "hiking." One of the blessed virtues of hiking, walking across the moors or along a country lane, is the great and healing boon of letting the mind go slack, letting the normal excitements of thought and planning and competitiveness and striving for excellence just go hang.

But the third type of boredom is very different: it might be called the boredom of ignorance. Because one has neither the curiosity nor the competence to understand a subject or to follow an argument, one becomes restless and professes to find it dull. Sometimes people are bored because they will not bother to try to understand what is going on. I recall a youth in a boys' club I once ran in East London. Whenever we had a speaker or a discussion group, he used to slink out the door. "You make use of the pool table and the football team and the canteen," I used to say gently, "why not stay for the meeting?" "Honest, sir," was the anguished reply, "thinking about religion just gives me a blooming headache!" Thinking of any sort bores some people.

I sometimes call this kind of boredom fake boredom, because deep down many people who suffer from it wish they did understand. They affect boredom to conceal their sense of inadequacy.

And so we come to the fourth type of boredom, which is necessary boredom. Tennyson said, "We needs must love the highest when we see it." But he was wrong; we needs must do nothing of the sort. For the highest always demands concentration, application, and perspiration. The greatest things in art and life do not offer their rewards without a corresponding effort. What is immediately attractive and easy to understand is generally third-rate. To enter into possession of great literature, great music, great art, I have had to endure a lot of preliminary boredom because, generally speaking, my natural taste was for lollipops and lemonade, for chocolate-box art and detective stories. Greatness in any area demands application, an educated palate, a maturity of judgment that is not easily acquired. The willingness to be bored is, in my opinion, a necessary ingredient of any growing life, if only as a spur to character!

But finally let us turn to the fifth and really serious form of boredom. The other four are in some ways necessary and inevitable. This one is boredom in its very essence.

Let me pinpoint it by two quotations. One is from *Trivia* by Logan Pearsall Smith. Logan's mother, Hannah Smith, was the author of a famous inspirational best seller, *The Christian's Secret of a Happy Life.* The boy rebelled against the intense evangelicalism of his home and became an agnostic. But in later life he wrote in his journal, "What a bore it is, waking up every morning the same old person!" That's boredom indeed, in its very root and flower—disgust at the sameness and staleness of one's own personality! The other sentence is equally illuminating, and it too comes from a diary—the *Journal* of André Gide, the French author. Writing about his visit to Italy, he records, "I found Rome most boring, but that was because I did not find myself interesting there." That cuts to the heart of things—one is bored because one is weary of oneself.

And why? Why do some people fail to find themselves interesting? First and foremost because nobody is interesting who is not interested. I once heard Canon Charles Raven say to a student audience, "I pity the man who does not find God more interesting than his own soul." He himself was a fascinating person because, being both a doctor of theology and a doctor of science, he was fascinated by the Creator as seen in his works and counted it all joy to "trace his pathway in the sea, his footsteps in the storm." He regarded the world not as a mirror in which to gaze at his own face, but a window through which to see God.

Second, nobody is interesting who is not growing. There are many things in the works of Aristotle I do not understand, but one sentence becomes more illuminating to me as the years pass: "Being is becoming." Vitality and interest depend on development and change—development from simple to complex, and back to simplicity again; development from material to spiritual, and back to the material again with a new grasp of it. Boring people—people who bore themselves—have usually stopped growing. And sometimes they wonder why life is so "weary, stale, flat, and unprofitable," and why religion and worship have lost their grip upon them. Is it not because they have not had a new thought for years, because they have not cracked their minds open with a new thought? Is it not because they have ceased to develop, and now spend all their time preserving the image they have built up or securing the gains they have made?

But more fundamentally, interesting people are persons who are more concerned to be real than to be interesting. The most deadly thing in the world is unreality. If I am asked, Have you never been bored? I have to answer in all honesty, Yes. But always the boredom has sprung from unreality—either in others or in myself. I have been bored by movies that had nothing to say; bored by conversations that were simply the echo of the daily newspaper; bored by windy preaching that was nothing but words about words; bored, above all, when I myself was evasive instead of honest, when I engaged in busywork that simply filled time without occupying it. But I have never been bored by a task, however difficult, that challenged me, or by a person, however limited and inarticulate, who was a real person.

Jesus is reported to have said, "You will know the truth, and the truth will make you free." To be alert to reality, to be constantly responding to the real, is the only way to escape vitiating boredom. I cannot possibly imagine Jesus being bored, for the reason that he was ever open to the claims and fascination of the real, forever alive to people at their deepest level.

stopping half way

*No one who puts his hand to the plow
and looks back is fit for the kingdom of
God.*

—LUKE 9:62

Such a man is not fit for any kingdom, much less for
the kingdom of God—whatever that means. Let's say it
means life—full, rich, abundant life, here and hereafter.

What is it that spoils life for many of us? Isn't it
that again and again we fail to follow through? That we
stop half way? Much of the trouble in the world today is
due not to bad men, but to good men who are just not
good enough. It comes not from false ideas, but from
true ideas that are only half worked out and then aban-
doned. The world is full of nice people, and yet it's in a
hell of a mess because nice people are simply not tough

enough, ruthless enough in their goodness to carry it to completion.

Consider the man Jesus was talking about in his parable. He had been over the field with his plow, he had scratched the surface of it, and then, just as things were getting interesting and exciting, he decided to call it a day. So there was the ground, good for nothing, in a worried and broken-up state, neither good building land nor a fully sown meadow—just a spoiled field.

Some people have just enough religion to spoil them as human beings. They are neither good, healthy pagans nor fully committed Christians, but a muddled mixture of both. The rewards of the Christian life come on the further side of the half way line. But how few of us reach it! We may have had one or two disturbing experiences—the hard, caked surface of life has been broken up—but then, instead of following through, we get either tired or frightened and abandon the plow.

We are hearing much in these days about school dropouts. It is a sorry state of affairs when a youngster has spent years of his life preparing to go forward and then abandons the whole project when, with a little extra effort, he could capitalize on all that time spent in the classroom. One final push of the plow and he might reap the harvest. Incidentally, this image of the plow is particularly applicable to education, for what is education in its early stages but the hard grind of opening up the soil to receive the seed? I stress the grind, because we have done a great disservice to young people by encouraging them to believe that everything must be interesting and that what is not immediately interesting is not worth knowing. There is nothing interesting about learning French irregular verbs, but without that hard slogging there is not much possibility of jabbering away to a French waiter in Paris. A boy may never do that, of course, but wouldn't it be a pity to get within sight of that and then abandon it, and so to have had all the hardship and none of the fun?

But even more serious than school dropouts are dropouts from life. And there are more of them! Countless grown-ups have done all the preliminary exercises and then have failed to utilize them. Let me be specific about this. Let me parade a few people before you.

Here is John Smith. All his life John has been a hard worker, but somewhere in middle life he has become discouraged. Because of middle-age mental spread, or because he never did have a clear idea of what he wanted from life in the first place, he has become fainthearted. He is neither in nor out of his job. He stands, as it were, in the middle of the field, dejected and ineffective.

Many a man reaches that point. Sometimes in desperation he throws the plow down and leaves the scene to seek "fresh woods and pastures new." It takes courage to do that. Sometimes it is the only sensible thing to do. It is better to waste half a life than to waste all of it. But the question arises: Why waste any of it? It is my observation that most men give in too easily and too soon. If, instead of turning back, they had pushed forward another few inches, they would have been within sight of victory. Even if they had not gone forward, had they gone deeper they might have discovered treasure. But instead of that, they got stuck. I know of no man who has yet fully exhausted the possibilities of any situation either in business or in personal life.

But let us bring the second man on the scene. Henry Robinson has, with determination and push, brilliantly exploited the possibilities of his business. He has made a resounding success of his vocation. But his marriage is a mess. He expected that to succeed without any effort on his part. He certainly put his hand to the plow, but then he expected it to proceed of its own volition. He has come to the point where he is now looking back and wondering whether he ought not to abandon the project altogether. But thanks to a wise friend he has come to see that the real trouble with his marriage is that he has simply scratched the surface of it. He has neither fully explored it nor given himself unreservedly to it.

And it has come to him that the same thing is true of another unsatisfactory area of his life—his religion. Here too he had put his hand to the plow and for a time made hard work of it. He did all the right things. He tithed, he toiled, he trod the straight and narrow path. He was trying to do Christian things without being a Christian.

He saw now that, because he had not penetrated to the depths of the religious life, he was trying to practice the precepts of Christianity without relating himself to its founder. And so his religion had become a matter of duty, not of delight; of strenuous obligation, not of joyful acceptance. He was trying to satisfy and salve his conscience, not to relate his soul to its Author and Owner.

There is an injunction in the Gospels that we should go the second mile. Very few Christians do that. Sometimes I wonder whether they should even try! It will only add to the burden of their guilt. It would be better and more realistic to complete the first mile, really and truly to cover that ground instead of stopping half way.

Let us bring the third man on the scene. The trouble with Tom Brown is that he has failed to follow through on his troubles. And he has had plenty of them, more than his share he thinks. Paul evidently had this man in mind when he asked, "Did you experience so many things in vain?" For the tragedy in many a life is not the suffering, but the suffering that yields no meaning. There is a line in T. S. Eliot that runs, "We have had the experience, but we have missed the meaning." This is what Paul means by experiencing "in vain." The experience of suffering for Tom Brown is not merely empty, however; it has soured and embittered his life; it has severed the nerve of action.

If I could I would like to introduce Tom to a lady I had the privilege of knowing some years ago. She was the mother of three boys in whom she took great pride. But the apple of her eye was the youngest, a lad of seventeen. Norman was not only a clever student, destined for a medical career; he was also a blithe spirit, all fire and air, made of some finer stuff than the rest of us. And then suddenly he was taken away; he was stricken with cerebral meningitis. I have never seen a woman respond with such magnificent courage to a blighted hope. Indeed, instead of breaking down under the blow, she seemed to draw upon hidden springs. From that moment on she dedicated herself more fully than before to the causes dear to her heart. And this was no passing thing, for it happened twenty years ago. Far from putting down the plow and looking back, she has gone forward to make a garden of life and to wrest from sorrow all that sorrow has to teach.

But let me bring on my final witness. Let us call him David Gray, for that would describe his outlook. David sees the future through a gray mist. It seems to him fraught with frightening perils and dangers. He has seen man put his hand to the plow and produce the most fantastic development of human power and mastery ever experienced. But he is not excited by it except in a negative way. He wishes there were some way of turning the hands of the clock back and of halting the progress of the plow, which to his mind has become a juggernaut.

Strangely enough, he is not an old man. There might be some excuse for that. He is a member of the college generation, but already he wants to contract out. Way back in the 'thirties, Lincoln Steffens came back from Russia and cried, "I have seen the future and it works!" Many of the younger generation can only cry, "We have seen the future and it stinks!" Like the Luddites in nineteenth-century England, they look at technological development with fear and loathing and are willing to throw a wrench into the works. Far from rising to the challenge of the new day, with its enormous potentiality for the uplift and welfare of the human family, they contract out by way of LSD and other drugs—like sex, for instance.

It is one of the great virtues of the French scientist-philosopher-saint, Pierre Teilhard de Chardin, that he steadfastly refused to be frightened of the future. With deeper penetration than Steffens he too has "seen the future and it works," if man will take up the plow and drive forward with confidence. But man must become man. Man must grow up. There is new ground beckoning him. He has inherited a new environment, no longer nature but nurture. If man stops half way with conquering nature, he has done only half the job. He must press on to give the same drive and determination to occupying the "noosphere"—that is, the environment created by his own thought and spirit—else he will lose all.

Robert Browning, for whom God be thanked, lived in an age of transition when hearts were fainting. How badly we need to hearken to his voice:

> Grow old along with me! The best is yet to be,
> The last of life, for which the first was made.

discourtesy

Love is not arrogant or rude.

—I CORINTHIANS 13:4

There are two great love poems in the Bible. The Song of Solomon in the Old Testament and Paul's Hymn of Love in the New Testament. One is a frank and beautiful celebration of physical love; the other is an equally beautiful but deeper description of what it means to love with the whole personality and to extend that love beyond the single individual to all men.

But the two poems have one thing in common. Both Solomon and Paul pause in mid-flight to warn us that love, like life, is made up of little things and can be destroyed by little things. Solomon puts it in a vivid image when he counsels the lover that the garden of love may be destroyed by the little foxes that sneak in unobserved among the vines. The most intense of romantic love affairs may be spoiled by apparently trivial habits, careless gestures, and casual discourtesies. Paul puts the same point in more positive form and in more direct language. Love is built up of commonplace virtues. It is "patient and kind, . . . not jealous or boastful, . . . not arrogant or rude, . . . not irritable or resentful."

"Love is not rude," says Paul flatly. But of course he is describing an ideal condition. In everyday practice, love is frequently rude. How often, after the first flush of marriage, two people neglect to observe the elementary courtesies of life! They are undeniably still in love, but they grow careless about the little gestures and sensitivities that once graced their relationship. Home becomes the place where, as the saying goes, they can "let down their hair"—or even come to breakfast with their hair in rollers! They no longer bother to keep up appearances. They use domesticity as a safety valve, to blow off steam. They reserve their party manners for parties. For one crime of passion there are a hundred acts of simple impoliteness, of childish sullenness, and of trivial irresponsibility; and these, in the end, wreak great havoc. Like little foxes these things creep in among the vines, and like the foxes often go unobserved by the people who are responsible for their entry.

It might be useful, therefore, to try to analyze this phenomenon of rudeness. For though small, it is not simple. It is possible to distinguish at least three kinds—deliberate, accidental, and unconscious.

Somebody once described a gentleman as a man who is never rude—except intentionally! And are there not occasions in life—not many, but some—when it is necessary to be rude and to act with calculated discourtesy? I hesitate to say this, because many people need no encouragement in this direction. But there are others who are too polite and lack the forthrightness to say, when the occasion demands it, "You are a fool! You are a knave!" In the face of deliberate cruelty, or reckless folly, or stupid behavior, one is not playing the part of a gentleman by saying politely, "Excuse me, sir, don't you think you're overdoing it? May I suggest tentatively that the little child you are beating up is entitled to human rights?"

There are opinions that are so outrageous and misinformed that the only possible response to them is "Rubbish!" Recently I read the report of an interview with the veteran theologian Reinhold Niebuhr. He was asked his opinion of those highly publicized thinkers, the "God is dead" theologians. He answered forthrightly, "I think they are stupid." Now that was certainly not very polite. And in fact many others have made the same estimate, and they *were* rude, for on their lips the opinion was that and nothing more—a rude and angry noise. But on Niebuhr's lips it was calculated rudeness, spoken in the interest of truth and backed up by clear and clearly expressed reasons. "I think they are stupid," said Niebuhr, "because they do not realize that all religious affirmations are symbolic, . . . because they have no system of coherence, . . . because they have neither digested the age-old problems of Christology nor understood what existentialism means." We may not agree with Niebuhr's reasons, but at least they are reasons and not reactions. I think that Niebuhr was being calculatedly rude, but there is a difference between shock treatment that is informed and reasonable and deliberate rudeness that is merely emotional.

Let's turn now to the second kind of rudeness—the accidental sort, as when one hurts the feelings and susceptibilities of others without even knowing it. But nine times out of ten, we should have known it. That's the point! It is part of the gentleness of a gentleman to be aware. People who pride themselves on their good manners, who would not be caught dead using the wrong fork or going through a door before a lady, are gauche and awkward in this sense—that they are not sufficiently interested in people to find out how they feel, and so are guilty of blundering roughshod into peoples' lives and of opening old wounds that they did not know existed.

Because we are not omniscient, we all do this at times. But when this happens, how many of us take steps to make immediate redress by the simple expedient of saying, "I'm sorry"?

But let us turn now to the third and most "foxy" kind of rudeness—unconscious rudeness. I am not writing now of such elementary breaches of decorum as coughing in people's faces, or sniffing instead of using a handkerchief, or yawning when people are speaking to you, or interrupting other people's conversation— although these are common enough. I mean by unconscious rudeness the preoccupation with oneself that rides brutally and blatantly over the feelings, the desires, the fears, and hopes of others.

It is said that "politeness costs nothing." It's a lie! Try being polite on a telegram or transatlantic cable; you will soon find out that every "please" and "thank you" sends your bill soaring. But in a deeper sense than that, politeness is always a costly business. Courtesy means taking pains. It means taking the trouble to see things from another's point of view. It demands the exercise of care over what you say and, even more important on occasions, how you say it. One man can say "thank you" in such a way that you feel insulted. What a lot there is in the tone of voice! One man can give an order so that your back arches immediately; another can give the same order in such a way that you feel honored to be the recipient of it.

As an example of unconscious rudeness, arising out of insensitivity, let me give a sample of what I mean. Take our thoughtless use of the word "Christian" to denote anything and everything which we think is good and right. "Why, the thing is unchristian!" we say. And in the nice, cosy community of WASPs everybody knows and accepts what we mean. But we are, after all, living in a pluralistic society, where our immediate neighbors may be Christian, Jewish, or agnostic. How do they feel when we arrogate to ourselves all the virtues? I always feel a shudder of revulsion when, at a public banquet or at a civic meeting attended by men of all faiths, I hear the clergyman who has been invited to give the invocation calling down God's blessing in the name of his Lord Jesus Christ. Would it not be more courteous, in such a mixed gathering, to call upon the God and Father of us all and to stress in the prayer the convictions we hold in common? This may seem a small and trivial instance, but it is a symptom of the unconscious rudeness that reveals a basic arrogance, an underlying contempt for the convictions and feelings of others, that mars the social fabric.

There is verse in the Old Testament, not important in itself yet very suggestive and, curiously enough, associated with that same Solomon who talked about the little foxes. When Solomon was building the temple in Jerusalem, he commanded that at the top of the pillars there should be lily work. Architecturally he may have been old-fashioned. In these days when architecture strives to be functional, when a house has been described as "a machine to live in," extraneous ornament is out.

But in matters of living and morals, such "lily work" improves life. It is the first function of a pillar to be strong, to stand erect and straight without crack or weakness. But sheer strength is not enough. Character without charm, principles without politeness, guts without grace, are not enough.

It is a pity that we do not possess a recording of Paul's Hymn of Love spoken by the author. But in its absence I make bold to suggest that the stress in the verse, "Love is not rude," fell on the first word. It is *love* that is not rude. Good manners and gracious living spring from love, that love which, as Paul was at pains to spell out, is no mere emotion, no gush of feeling, but an orientation of the whole personality toward the good of others, a steady resolve to live with people at such a depth that they are encouraged to be their truest and deepest selves.

I Corinthians 13, as has often been pointed out, reads like a word portrait of Jesus Christ. With no diminution at all—in fact with great enrichment—it could, with the substitution of "Jesus Christ" for "love," give us the best description we possess of the Lord Christ in his habit as he lived. Would that we could take the further step and so live "in Christ" that men would be moved to substitute for "love" the name "Christian"!

flippancy

But they made light of it.

—MATTHEW 22:5

One of the most mischievous despoilers of the vines I know is really a combination of fox and laughing hyena. His name is "flippancy." But let me be quick to point out that flippancy is not the same as humor. "Anything for a laugh" is not the same as "seeing the funny side of things." Flippancy is seeing the funny side of things that have no funny side. Humor is God's gift to disinfect the world of pomposity. A sense of humor is nothing more or less than a sense of proportion— especially a sense of proportion about oneself.

This came home to me recently as I listened to a lecture by a well-known author whose books, for some reason or other, have always fascinated me although I dislike them. I had never been able to put my finger on the reason until I heard him speak in public, and then it came to me in a flash. The man has no sense of humor. Oh, yes, he told a funny story and cracked a few jokes— but humor? Not a vestige. He talked, among other things, about his religion, which was a combination of Zen Buddhism, private mysticism, and intellectual snobbery. As I came out I said to a friend, "Now I know why I am a Christian! Now I know why I believe in the religion of the Incarnation. Because it delivers me from all that pomposity about myself." Christianity, thank God, is not about ideas, concepts, philosophies, and feelings: it's about a man. God's word is made flesh. And the Christian life is not a soul trying to fly through space; it's a way of eating, drinking, making love, patting little children on the head, frying fish over an open fire for hungry disciples.

God has a sense of humor. Why else should there be monkeys, dromedaries—and ducks. "Ducks are comical things," as the poet says:

When God had finished the stars and whirl of coloured
  suns
He turned His mind from big things to fashion little ones,
Beautiful tiny things (like daisies) He made, and then
He made the comical ones in case the minds of men
            Should stiffen and become
            Dull, humourless and glum:
And so forgetful of their Maker be
As to take even themselves—*quite seriously.*

The only thing wrong with that verse is that the poet should have said "solemnly" instead of "seriously." A man should take himself seriously, but that is a very different thing from solemnity. To be solemn is to be pompous, to stand on one's dignity—a very slippery place on which to stand. It is to dramatize oneself as—of all absurdities!—a "seeker after God," when the plain truth is that most of us are dodging God, like Adam in the garden, like Jonah taking ship to Tarshish.

But flippancy—now, that's something else again. A flippant person is frivolous, a man who is determined to make a joke of everything, even when there is no joke.

In that sprightly modern classic *The Screwtape Letters*, C. S. Lewis warned us all against the wiles of the devil. One of the most effective weapons in the devil's armory is to instill into people a misplaced sense of humor. Two people have recently become converted to Christianity. Naturally the devil is disturbed about this, but he sees hope on the horizon, for he notes that they have fallen in with a set who are great comics, who will do anything to get a laugh. As long as they are consorting with flippant people, he says, there is still hope of their damnation. For flippancy is essentially a way of evading the truth and of covering up the unpleasant and unpalatable. When a man makes a joke of everything, he manages to cover up the shame of what is shameful.

So, if a man habitually lets others pay for him, he is tightfisted; but if he boasts about it in a jocular manner and taunts his victims with having been outwitted, he is no longer a mean skinflint—he is a comical chap! Again, cowardice is shameful, but cowardice boasted off with humorous exaggeration will pass muster. For one purpose of flippancy is to disguise the harsh outlines of things.

But there is another side to this. While some people express their flippancy by giving pleasant names to ugly things, others do it by giving ugly names to pleasant things. They downgrade and devalue the precious and lovely things of life by the use of bad language and obscenity. The vocabulary they employ vulgarizes and cheapens the sanctities of love, the ecstasies of religion, and the grace of life. It leaves a trail of slime on everything it touches. Sometimes I think this is why people swear and make dirty jokes—not because they feel funny about certain subjects, but because they feel frightened of them. Because they do not want to be involved at too deep a level, they become flippant about the high mutualities of married love. They deliberately use the divine Name as an oath to blunt its impact. They are unconsciously trying to deaden their sensitivity to truth and beauty and goodness, in order that they may not be got at.

But it is possible to "make light of it" without using bad language. Some whose tongues are perfectly clean are flippant at the very center of their souls. They reveal this flippancy in their disregard of truth. It is not that they tell lies, but that they do not trust truth to carry its own weight. Paul Goodman tells how he was commissioned by the editor of a famous magazine to write an article. When Goodman showed it to him, he was told: "We can't use that. You can't expect our readers to think. Do it again. Jazz it up; you know how—the apt illustration, the alarming statistic." Goodman's comment was, "The most alarming statistic I know is the circulation of that particular magazine!" Anything is alarming that does not take truth seriously and that refuses to take people more seriously than they take themselves—art, literature, advertising, even preaching!

It is one of the charges brought by some Roman Catholics against their Church. The Catholic theologian, Canon Charles Davis, left the Church because its attitude to truth was essentially flippant. "There is concern for authority at the expense of truth," he declared. "The official Church is racked by fear, insecurity and anxiety with a consequent intolerance and lack of love." And many of those, who in spite of their deep dissatisfaction remain within the Church, echo his charge. You cannot play fast and loose with truth, even to bolster up a beloved institution. Davis speaks of the "callous dishonesty of the Pope's postponement in October, 1967 of a decision on birth control," an issue that is in the opinion of many Catholics "tearing family life apart." It may seem strange to talk about flippancy in this connection, where the issues are so grave and the problems so momentous, but no other word seems to fit when the considerations of order, authority, and the safety of an institution are allowed to take precedence over the welfare and integrity of the human person.

But Protestants have their own brand of flippancy also. I once heard that craggy, suggestive thinker, Eugen Rosenstock-Huessy, author of *The Christian Future,* cry out against what he called "playing games." So few people, he declared, in American Protestantism are serious about their religion. And isn't this one reason for the constant drain from the ministry? Many people in our churches would be shocked if they realized how many ministers have left the pastorate in recent years: some because they were forced out as a result of their stand on civil rights or some other controversial issue; some because they have departed for positions as social workers, or as chaplains in hospitals, in industry and on college campuses. When you ask them why, they say it is because the local congregation is the very last place where religion is taken seriously. The average church member, such is their charge, is intent on miniaturizing everything—turning the Savior of the world into my personal savior, reducing salvation to safety and Christian witness to "being kind to granny and the cat."

But back to the text! The people who "made light of it" were the men in Christ's parable who were invited to a royal wedding feast. They were asked to the party, but one by one they began to make excuses. And what excuses! Essentially frivolous ones. One said he had bought a field and had to inspect it. At night! What a joke! One said he had bought five yoke of oxen and had to go and try them out. At night! And one had married a wife—period. One can hear the great guffaw that greeted that excuse.

Yet the point of the parable is plain. Life offered these men an opportunity for joy, and they passed it up. For this is the real tragedy of flippancy, not that it shuts us out from such onerous and ponderous things as duty, service, responsibility, and sacrifice, but that it shuts us out from joy. Only the serious man can thoroughly enjoy himself. Only the man who has a hard day's work behind him can know the pleasure of relaxing. To take up a frivolous attitude to life is to miss its greatest rewards. But more, it is to distort one's relationship to reality and so to curtail one's own usefulness and availability to God.

There are some things that one dare not take lightly. Great art, great literature, great music, great living all proceed from facing, not evading, the issues of life. As Faulkner said of literature, in accepting the Nobel Prize, "The only thing worth the sweat and agony of writing is the human heart in conflict with itself. If the writer forgets this he labors under a curse, he writes not of love but of lust, of defeats in which nobody loses anything of any value, of victories without hope. He writes not of the heart but of the glands."

shadowboxing

*Well, I do not run aimlessly, I do not
box as one beating the air.*

—I CORINTHIANS 9:26

One of the greatest of all life-wasters and life-spoilers
is misplaced energy. Paul puts it in an unforgettable
picture: "Well, I do not run aimlessly, I do not box as
one beating the air."

It may take more imagination than some of us possess
to envisage Paul in running shorts and boxing gloves!
But in fact, isn't it astonishing how often in the course
of his letters he throws out these casual references to
the world of sport—to the arena, the racetrack, the
wrestling match, the chariot race, and the boxing ring?

A man does not refer to these things in passing unless
he is familiar with them and interested in them. I am
not suggesting that Paul was a participant, but he certainly sounded like a spectator, if not a fan. And if this

is true, does it not throw a fascinating sidelight on the character of the man? We are inclined to regard him as a somewhat wan and sickly scholar, endlessly debating points of theology. But the touchline, the finish wire, and the stadium have in his writings a place alongside the Old Testament and the rabbis. Maybe it is possible to make too much of this, but it is not unimportant for an understanding of Paul and of his theology. Is it possible that interpreters have put too much emphasis on his references to the law court and the slave market, and so produced a Pauline theology that is legalistic and even vindictive? Had they paid more attention to the sporting terms, they might have received another impression of the Christian life—not as a dodging of penalties from a judge on the bench, but as a striving to win applause from a judge in the box! They might have seen that Paul dramatized life as a game and as an exciting and dynamic struggle.

William James speaks like Paul when he says, "If this life be not a real fight, in which something is eternally gained for the universe by success, it is no better than a game of private theatricals from which we may withdraw at will. But it *feels* like a real fight." It certainly felt like that to Paul, and it is in these terms that he loved to speak of it. So run that you might obtain! So fight that you put your fist where it counts!

There were evidently people in Corinth who were running about with great vigor but going nowhere in particular. They were indulging in a lot of fancy foot-work, lunging, and muscle-flexing, but all the feinting and sparring and sidestepping—especially the sidestep-ping—were taking place in the gymnasium and not in the ring. They were fighting, not real enemies but their own shadows, or shadows of enemies who had once existed but had now disappeared. And this kind of shadowboxing is not unknown in our own time and in America.

Some time ago an article with the alarming title "To Hell with the Church!" was published in a religious periodical. Many conventional Christians were horrified by this title. But is not that exactly where the church should go—to hell? William Booth, the founder of the Salvation Army, evidently thought so, for did he not say in explanation of his movement, "I hungered for hell"? He passionately desired to be where evil was most rampant, where there was wrong to be righted, evil to be fought. He chose as his opponents the ugliest and the most challenging of foes. But many of us simply do not have the spiritual energy to go to hell, although Christ promised his disciples that the gates of hell should not prevail against them.

Let us glance at two specific things that deflected the energy of those old Corinthian Christians. One was the very intensity of their loyalty, although it was loyalty in the wrong place. "It has been reported to me," writes Paul, "that there is quarreling among you, my brethren.

What I mean is that each one of you says, 'I belong to Paul,' or 'I belong to Apollos,' or 'I belong to Cephas.'" Maybe these are just names to us. Paul we have certainly heard of. Cephas? Well, isn't that another version of Peter? About Apollos we hear that he was popular with certain intellectuals, for he was the scholar-preacher, the philosopher, the speaker to the "cultured despisers." These men differed in many respects, but they shared a common aim—to exalt Christ. Their followers, however, were more intent on exalting them! And that situation is not unknown today. For are there not those among us who say, "I belong to Barth," or "I belong to Bultmann," or "I belong to Tillich"? I am sure that there are very real issues at stake here, but I also wonder about the energy that goes into theological debate. Are we not in some danger of sparring among ourselves instead of keeping a steady eye on the real enemy?

Another form that "shadowboxing" took in ancient Corinth was internal rivalry in the church. Specifically it took the form of boasting about "tongues," the ability to go off into a kind of spiritual trance. There was a strong pentecostal element in the early church. It was regarded by many as a sign of spiritual superiority to be able to break into ecstatic utterance. It was a proof that one was in the grip of the Spirit. The issue became so acute that there were actually two parties within the fellowship—one contending that no man was a Christian unless he could talk nonsense! I mean that literally, for speaking in tongues made no sense; it was simply a badge of the "in" group.

Paul got very angry about this. "I thank God that I speak in tongues more than you all," he cried. "Nevertheless, in church I would rather speak five words with my mind, in order to instruct others, than ten thousand words in a tongue." And one would have thought that that would be the end of the matter. But it was not so. The debate continued. For poor, weak, energy-squandering human nature is forever prone to look for some outward sign to assure itself that it is in a special class. To this very day there are people who are quick to classify their fellow-Christians according to some gift, some pattern of belief or behavior, and to exalt this as the sole criterion for being "in" the Christian family. It may be tongues; it may be baptism—or some special form of it; it may be conversion—according to one standardized pattern; it may be subscription to a creed or a proper form of words. In any case, far too much spiritual energy goes into this kind of thing, energy that would be more profitably employed in striving to outdo one another in loving, learning, and living.

But in this twentieth century there are forms of spiritual shadowboxing peculiar to our age. One of them is our failure to recognize that the enemy has been overcome, or that he has moved on, or that another and more deadly enemy has taken his place. We are often guilty, in both our personal and our church lives, of sparring with opponents who are no longer there. In his intellectual and spiritual autobiography Max Planck, the Nobel Prize winner, wrote a chapter which he entitled, "Phantom Problems in Physics." Are there not phantom problems in every area of life? The old struggle between science and religion may be one of them. That problem in its nineteenth-century form has ceased to be a real problem. Many thinking men agree today with Albert Einstein that "science at its greatest is identical with religion at its most sublime," and that "without deep faith in the rationality of the world there would have been no science." It seems to me that where there is a struggle today, it is a sham battle between bad religion and bad science.

And all the time there is a real battle to be fought. But it is not so much between science and religion as between reverence and exploitation; it is between the religious and the irreligious use of science. In particular, it is a struggle against what applied science is *doing* to us. We have to be on guard all the time against the practical results of science lest those results so enthrall us that we are diverted from asking the real questions of life. Today we are so bemused by the abundance of gadgets and gimmickery that we can pass a lifetime manipulating them and so postponing coming to terms with ourselves. The arena has shifted; it is no longer theoretical but practical. We are in danger of being manipulated by those who have seized control of the machinery and resources of science. Technological advances have enabled them not merely to increase the number of products and to advertise them on a large scale, but to inflame our greed for them, to shape our wants, and to turn us into customers—consumers of everything and anything just because it is there. Not only is the product being shaped to fit the customer; the customer is being shaped to fit the product. We have to be alert to every effort to destroy our individuality, our powers of discrimination, and our sense of values.

But let me return to the personal aspect of all this, for it is in the realm of the personality that shadowboxing is most rife. Some of us sometimes wonder why the personal moral struggle, the battle with our own sins, goes so badly with us. May it not be that we are fighting the wrong enemy? William James once laid it down as a law that "when the will and the imagination are in conflict, the imagination always wins." In spite of this we go on fighting the bad will, clenching our fists and tensing our muscles, when all the time the real enemy is winning his fight in the chambers of the imagination, which we are doing little to enrich and fortify with positive and glowing symbols and pictures. Recall that he who said he was no shadow boxer also advised his converts, "Consider yourselves dead to sin and alive to God." In other words, do not empty your mind; populate it so thickly with images, with thoughts of "whatever is lovely, whatever is gracious," that there will be no room for temptation, save only the greatest temptation of all—the temptation to be great and greatly good after that mind which was in Christ Jesus.

prisoners
of hope

*Return to your stronghold, O prisoners
of hope.*

—ZECHARIAH 9:12

What an extraordinary phrase—"prisoners of hope"!
Is not hope always a liberating thing? Despair and hope-
lessness can imprison men, but hope? Surely not. Yet
here is the little-heeded prophet Zechariah maintaining
that hope may take man prisoner too. When I first read
his words, they pulled me up short. I didn't quite know
what to do with them, so I jotted them down in my
notebook; and there they remained for a couple of years,
just a sentence heading an otherwise empty page,
awaiting comment.

One day, rereading Dickens, I remembered Mr.

Micawber, who was always "waiting for something to turn up." There was a prisoner of hope! Wilkins Micawber was so full of hope, so focused on the future, that he landed in jail, the famous Marshalsea Prison for debtors.

A few months passed. One day I saw in a daily newspaper that Mr. Aneurin Bevan, the British health minister, had been on a visit to Russia. As he stepped off the plane at London Airport, he was asked for his impressions. He answered, "My chief impression is, that while we in Britain may be slaves to the past, in Russia they are slaves to the future." Prisoners of hope again!

Recently I went to see the movie *Ship of Fools*. This is one of those rare films that is better than the book. Katherine Ann Porter's novel floored me; I just could not finish it. But the film is a different matter. What got lost in a maze of words in the book emerged with splendid clarity in the film. Who are the fools in *Ship of Fools?* They are not stupid men and women, but people hypnotized by hope—hope without foundation in fact or reality. They are people deluded, driven crazy by hope without substance. They all, in one way or another, hope to make a comeback—to a Germany that has passed away forever, to a youth that can never be recaptured, to a love that has died and cannot be resurrected.

Prisoners of hope! My notebook was filling up. Old Zechariah was being brought up to date. As he saw many centuries ago, not all hope is liberating. Some of it is confining and restrictive.

Imprisoning hope is unrealistic. There are hopes to which we pay lip service, though we know in our hearts that they cannot come to pass. Indeed, no one would be more surprised than we if they did come to pass. There was an item in a Jewish newspaper some while ago from which I learned that some congregations in America are agitating for a reform of the liturgy. At one of the lovely ceremonies of Judaism, the host lifts his glass at the end of the ritual meal and piously breathes the prayer, "Next year in Jerusalem!" As long as there was no real likelihood of this happening, this prayer had been pronounced with great fervor for centuries. But now that it is physically possible to go to Jerusalem, many discover that the prayer is an empty gesture.

There are Christian hopes that are just as unreal. Jesus once asked a man, "Do you want to be healed?" The man had assumed that this was the greatest hope of his life; yet when it was within his reach, he drew back. His whole manner of life for thirty-eight years had unfitted him to enter upon the healthy life he pretended to hope for.

As there are unrealistic hopes, so there are limited, halfway hopes, and these often take a man prisoner. We recall Augustine's famous prayer, "O Lord, give me chastity, but not yet!" Some of us have hopes that are equally limited. Recently a Baptist leader from Texas, addressing the Southern Baptist Convention, said, "I am not suggesting that we lightly cast aside our cherished Southern Way of Life. I am suggesting that we throw it aside with great vigor wherever it violates the spirit of the Bible." That is a well-deserved rebuke to those whose Christian hope stops short at some national or regional frontier.

And there is hope that imprisons a man because it is directed to the wrong object or an inadequate goal. In his novel *The Arrangement*, Elia Kazan, the well-known stage and film director, makes one of his characters say, "Adulthood lies in the acceptance of limited objectives in life." But the trouble with "limited objectives" is that we might attain them! And then what? We have all known men who have tried to fulfill life by concentrating on the limited goals of success in business, or domestic tranquillity, or local prominence, only to discover that they have brilliantly succeeded in "the worldly hopes men set their hearts upon" and have watched them, with Omar Khayyam, "turn ashes."

Yet having said all that, it is true that hope does keep man alive. A man with no interest in the future is only half a man. It is when the future blots out the present that he becomes imprisoned.

There is a compelling phrase in the Old Testament which runs, "The eyes of a fool are on the ends of the earth." That is where Mr. Micawber's eyes were, so fixed on the glories and bright promise of tomorrow that he neglected the duties and opportunities of this day. That is where Stalin's eyes were, so focused on the future freedom of humanity in the classless society that he was willing to subject men to actual imprisonment and even death. When protest was voiced against the brutalities and massacres of the regime, against the imprisonments, forced labor, and the suppression of truth, it was explained that it was all temporary, all done in the interest of the glorious future, for "you can't make omelets without breaking eggs!" Any hope in the future that makes us careless and contemptuous of the only reality we possess—the living present, which for the sake of some coming "good of humanity" compels us to ride roughshod over the rights and welfare of the present individual—is doomed to failure.

In the sphere of personal life, some kinds of hope can be confining and imprisoning. Somebody once said that the two saddest sentences in the world are "There's plenty of time yet" and "It's too late now." Many a young man has uttered the first, and the years roll by, the buoyancy of youth ebbs, and he wakes up one morning to realize that it's too late now. All that might have been is no longer possible; the doors of opportunity have closed upon him; the age limit has been passed. Hope in this case was a snare and a delusion; it lulled the young man into overconfidence. The future seemed a vast empty space waiting to be occupied, but now it has shrunk to nothing.

But the proverbial warning, "The eyes of a fool are on the ends of the earth," applies with peculiar relevance to religious people. We know there are religious sects whose eyes are so firmly fixed on the millennium that their heavenly religion is no earthly use, that all the interim between then and now is simply wasteland. Of what value is it, they ask, to engage in social work, to support the United Fund, to work for better government, to build schools and hospitals, if at any moment now the Lord will come with a shout and the sound of a trumpet to clear up the whole sad and sorry mess?

There is a large and growing sect whose slogan is "Millions now living will never die." Of greater concern to some of us is that millions now dying will never live. And this seems to us to be the concern of the New Testament. The most emphatic and important word in the New Testament is "now." "Now is the judgment of this world." "Now is the acceptable time." "We are God's children now; it does not yet appear what we shall be." "It is full time now for you to wake from sleep." Yes, the judgment is now, not in some far-off divine event, for every day is judgment day. "This is the judgment, that the light has come into the world, and men loved darkness rather than light." And now is the kingdom of Heaven present in our midst, the fullness of truth waiting to be appropriated, the splendor of goodness and beauty immediately available to us. And now are we the sons of God; it is now, not later, that the Father says, "Son, you are always with me and all that is mine is yours."

There is, of course, a paradox here. "The Lord has yet more light and truth to break forth from his holy word," as John Robinson has said. Yet it is also true that Christ is even now the fullest, finest, and final revelation of life's meaning and God's purpose. How can it be so, that Christ is at once both final and coming again? To make a human analogy: we know that there is a finality about the beauty of the Parthenon in architecture, about the portraits of Rembrandt in art, about the Beethoven symphonies in music. They are so full that they are inexhaustible; they yield ever-new meanings as life deepens us, as experience chastens us, and as love humanizes us. And is it not so with Christ? At every stage of life's way, he reveals ever more and more of himself. "The sea always grows greater." We paddle in it as children, we swim in it as adults, but it is the same sea.

A man who puts his hope in Christ is not locking himself into a premature and stifling loyalty. If he puts his hope in another human being, he often finds that he has bartered part of his freedom to the demands and limitations of the other person. But the greater the human being, the less likely is this to happen, for no truly great human being desires anything but the complete freedom of the other person to be himself, his richest and truest self. If a man puts himself at the service of a system or institution, he may discover that he is hedged in and enchained by the requirements of that system or organization. But the Christian commitment is to a person. It is to this "stronghold" that, in Zechariah's words, we must ever "return" if we are not to embark on the "ship of fools."

restlessness

*My people hath been lost sheep . . .
They have gone from mountain to hill,
they have forgotten their restingplace.*

—JEREMIAH 50:6 KJV

There was a parish minister in Scotland who used to say that in old age he read only two books, God's Book and the devil's—the Bible and a certain daily newspaper.

Sometimes they complement each other remarkably. This word from Jeremiah, for example, is well over two thousand years old, but it might have been lifted from this morning's headlines. "They have gone from mountain to hill, they have forgotten their restingplace" is a graphic description of those frenzied people in modern society who go scrambling from one peak of sensation to another; those crazy kids and their crash parties; those jaded society folk who, no longer titillated by normal sex, pant from one erotic thrill to another. Even the most normal of us are itching to be on the move, for this is a restless age in which we live. Jeremiah characterized it vividly: we have forgotten our restingplaces, and we are trying to compensate for the lack of inner stability by outer activity.

But there are two kinds of activity. There is activity that is the spontaneous overflow of abundance; and there is activity that is the artificial attempt to create abundance, or at least to fill up the emptiness. Creative activity is the natural expression of fullness of being; uncreative activity is a desperate attempt to pump up some kind of simulated life. In a recent novel an Italian priest is overheard to say, "You Americans think you need rest, but what you are actually seeking is peace." Behind and beneath modern man's search for excitement and distraction there is a wrong-headed attempt to find abiding satisfaction and a reason for living.

A man can stand a lot of boredom and routine if he knows the fundamental orientation of his life is right. The more deeply satisfying a man's job is, the less extrinsic excitement he craves. Every profession and trade has its stretches of sheer boring and monotonous routine; but if a man has a sense of vocation, he can absorb them. But where there is no sense of vocation, no dignity, or worthwhileness within his lifework, it has to be sought for in "kicks" and cookouts.

John Gunther's son Johnny, who was a better philosopher at seventeen when he died of meningitis than some of us will be at seventy, left behind a private notebook in which he jotted down one day the lines,

> Contentment with the universe.
> Discontent with the world.

If a person is at peace with the universe, at one with his Creator, attuned to reality, sure of his place and purpose within the large scheme of things, then he is free to be discontented, creatively discontented, with the domestic arrangements here on earth. If he is rooted in some central stabilities and nourished by a few great convictions, he can be profitably, even happily, discontented with things as they are. But if he is merely critical, merely dissatisfied, then he stands the risk of being merely edgy and querulous. When Robert Frost the poet came to die, he asked that there should be engraved on his tombstone the words, "I had a lover's quarrel with the world." He nagged and chided the world not, as too often happens, because he disliked it and distrusted it, but because he longed to see its rich possibilities realized, its promise fulfilled, and its goodness evoked. But then, you see, Robert Frost had not forgotten his restingplace. After a period of initial uncertainty, he had found his vocation. He knew what he had been called to do and so had no necessity to go scrambling from mountain to hill.

Jeremiah spoke of the restingplace of life. Without becoming pious about it, can we discern such restingplaces?

A man's work is certainly one of them. On a purely human plane I am not sure that this is not the greatest. Many men find a satisfaction and stability in work that they discover nowhere else. It is, normally speaking, a man's work that gives direction and drive and purpose to his daily existence—the joy of achievement, the challenge of the difficult, the fibers that run out from that work to relate him to others, the feeling that his job contributes to the common weal. Thomas Carlyle used to preach the gospel of work—a strange phrase to many a modern ear. Work is often regarded as a dreary, inescapable necessity by some. But Carlyle knew from bitter experience that there is gospel, good news, goodness, healing, and even salvation in work. When all human props collapse and sorrow devastates a man, his work will give him something to live for.

But it has to be work that really stretches him and that contributes to human dignity, not just busywork or a job that simply exploits human greed and cupidity. This is one reason why a young person should be careful about his choice of a trade or profession, not merely because he is going to be in it a long time, but because it is going to make him or break him and either bring him alive inside or disgust and deaden him. As Henry David Thoreau knew, a man is cheated if his work rewards him only with money wages. It should be the sort of work that pays him in life-wages—more liveliness of mind and heart, increasing skill—and brings him into a more meaningful relationship with his fellowmen.

Friendship is another great restingplace. Some years ago I heard the philosopher John McMurry deliver the Gifford Lectures in Scotland. I found it hard going to follow his close-knit argument. So when the lectures were printed, I turned to them eagerly, and lo! in the preface he had summarized twenty lectures in three lines. "All meaningful knowledge is for the sake of action. All meaningful action is for the sake of friendship." That, said the noted philosopher, is the goal of all our significant striving, to be capable of friendship, to be more available to one another, to be more generous and large-hearted human beings, and to be more richly related one to another.

Because many of us substitute friendliness for friendship, togetherness for community, or even try to construct a world bounded by envy and tightfisted exclusion, we only succeed in making a frantic world, a mountain-to-hill world, because envy and greed have no limit and give no ultimate satisfactions.

But in the end, of course, the great restingplace of life is religion. You would expect me to say that, naturally! But in fact I have to say it because it is the whole point of the text. Jeremiah was talking about religion. Indeed his words are a description of two kinds of religion—religions that stabilize and enrich life, and religions that merely agitate and eventually diminish it.

"They have gone from mountain to hill," said Jeremiah of certain of his compatriots, and although I am using his words figuratively, he was using them literally. In the historical context his words are not an analogy for frenzied living, neither was he speaking of metaphorical hills and mountains. He was referring to actual places on the map—those "high places" so frequently mentioned in the Old Testament, those mountain shrines dedicated to the old pagan gods, where people indulged in disgusting orgies and wild abandon and sought religious ecstasy by cutting themselves, by whipping up enthusiasm through erotic dancing, and by letting themselves go in every kind of riotous excess.

To his great sorrow, Jeremiah found his fellow countrymen sneaking off to these pagan altars. Officially they were Israelites, dedicated to the high, austere, moral worship of the One God, the God of truth and justice and mercy; but again and again their itching feet drove them to the hills for a religious jamboree, to seek ecstasy, release, excitement. Such a type of religion is not unknown even in modern America, and not only in the backhills of small, rural communities and among such sects as the snake-handlers and extreme pentecostalists. It is found also in more sophisticated form in every denomination where emotionalism, even such tepid emotionalism as hymn-singing (and how tepid that can be!), becomes a flight from reality rather than a facing of it, and where pleasant "religious" feelings do duty for dedication to the beloved community of which Christ is the center.

"Return to your restingplace!" cried Jeremiah. And that too is more than a metaphor. In fact it is almost a technical term in the Bible for the place where the Ark rested—that great box which the Israelites carried with them as a standing symbol of God's presence in their midst, and which contained the tables of the Law, the Ten Commandments, God's gracious gift to his covenant people as an everlasting reminder that God and man are indissolvably linked.

To put it contemporaneously, the restingplace of life is where man realizes and claims his personal relationship to his Creator, to whom he is bound not by "kicks" and feelings or religious emotionalism, but by God's covenant of love.

In Jesus Christ that covenant of love became flesh and dwelt among us, so that Jesus could say, "Come to me . . . and I will give you rest." You and I are called, not to be religious fun-chasers or spiritual dervishes dancing attendance at one ecclesiastical pep rally after another. "Life in Christ" offers us "content with the universe, discontent with the world"—both a wholesome, abiding satisfaction at being at one with God, and a life of significant struggle. A life attuned to God in Christ is, even in its ordinary moments, dramatic, since we are caught up in a play in which our small part counts and our smallest actions can be dedicated to the enlargement and triumph of love. Nothing is insignificant to the Christian man; every smallest decision is a call upon his integrity and obedience. And in Christ he is constantly being renewed, made a "new creation" in order that he may sally forth into each day's life to make all things new.

careless talk

Let the words of my mouth and the meditation of my heart be acceptable in thy sight, O Lord, my rock and my redeemer.

—PSALM 19:14

Seeing that we spend so much of our time talking—chatting with friends, transacting business, discussing the weather, criticizing the administration, talk, talk, talk from the time we get up until we go to bed (and sometimes after!)—it is odd that we hear so few sermons on the discipline of the tongue. We are all agreed that the Christian life is concerned with behavior. But what a large part of behavior consists simply of opening our mouths—in greeting, in giving advice, in expressing sympathy, voicing thanks, and in passing judgment. Words, words, words, from morning till night.

The Bible is well aware of this and contains many

warnings about careless talk. "Let the words of my mouth be acceptable in thy sight," cries the psalmist. And in another place, "Set a guard over my mouth, O Lord, keep watch over the door of my lips!" As for Jesus, some of the sternest things he ever said concerned the necessity for conversational discipline. "On the day of Judgment men will render account for every careless word they utter; for by your words you will be justified, and by your words you will be condemned." "Let what you say be simply 'Yes' or 'No'; anything more than this comes from evil." "Whoever insults his brother shall be liable to the council, and whoever says 'You fool!' shall be liable to the hell of fire."

My goodness! It's a wonder that any of us have the temerity to open our mouths at all. Yet open them we do, and how carelessly and glibly. We embark upon a conversation without the faintest idea where it is going to lead or what good or evil will come out of it.

It was said of Job by his so-called comforters, "Your words have kept men on their feet." Of how many of us can that be said? You and I often speak, quite unwittingly, words that knock men off their feet, that take the wind out of their sails, harsh words that deflate people and send them reeling.

What then can we do to cultivate careful talk, and to set a guard upon our lips?

First, we can talk less and listen more. Much of what we say in the course of a normal day is simply nervous chatter, designed more to avoid thought then to provoke it. We speak to cover up the discomfort of silence. We talk in order to avoid the embarrassment of boredom. This is very often the origin of gossip. A gossip is usually someone who indulges in tittle-tattle, usually vindictive; but the original meaning of gossip is one who stands sponsor at a christening—God's sib, a sibling in relation to God. The word has suffered the same fate as many other religious expressions. And it is notorious that many of these debased words have to do with speech. "Patter," for example, has now come to denote glib, mechanical speech that simply rattles on and on. It is of course a corruption of *pater noster*, the opening words of the Lord's Prayer in Latin. "Hocus pocus," meaning gibberish, is a slurred way of saying *Hoc est corpus* (this is my body), the most solemn words of the communion service.

When Jesus said, "Let what you say be simply 'Yes' or 'No'; anything more than this comes from evil," he knew from experience that the elaboration of truth is often its downfall, and that words are often used with no other intent than to save men the trouble of listening.

Second, we can talk positively. Much talk is 3-D talk—not three dimensional, but discouraging, disparaging, and downgrading. How often people, without intending it, discourage idealism and lively experiment. "It's all been tried before," they say when faced with a proposal, or "When you're my age, you will realize that things are not as simple as that." All very wise and true, no doubt, but not very helpful. In any case they fail to realize that though a thing has been tried before, it might have been tried by the wrong people and at the wrong time.

Disparaging talk is even more destructive. It has a sour note, it reduces all idealism to a subtle form of self-interest and discounts heroism by calling it exhibitionism. A journalist once told me that he had an infallible test for sounding out a man's character. Called to interview a politician, a parson, or a painter, he first asks him what he thinks of a fellow politician, another parson, a rival painter. Very few people pass that test with flying colors, he says. Even if they begin with compliments, they usually manage to get in some snide remark that suggests the other fellow is not all he is cracked up to be.

As for the downgraders and the degraders, they are found in every walk of life, and they leave a trail of slime on everything they touch. When you have finished talking to these gentlemen, you find that everything has been reduced to half its original size. Lytton Strachey was an expert at this. When he had finished with Florence Nightingale, she was no longer "the lady of the lamp" but a frustrated spinster. The Eminent Victorians, seen through his eyes, became a bunch of neurotics, secret drinkers, pompous hypocrites. But something else revealed itself in that infamous book—the tiny, shrivveled, desiccated soul of Lytton Strachey.

The third discipline we can exercise over the careless tongue is to cut out the bad language. I don't mean swear words. I mean those weasel words, those loaded terms that do nothing at all to clarify discussion or to promote truth but serve only to darken counsel and to inflame prejudice. The real dirty words are not the so-called obscenities, but such expressions as "wop," "nigger," "kike," "crackpot," "crank," and their tribe, words that are deeply charged with fear and hate.

Bad language is language that puts an end to discussion instead of opening it up. This is why slogans are dangerous, and especially religious slogans. They may be perfectly true, but they foreclose the issue. How often I have been in the midst of serious men, strenuously grappling with the problems of life, and then some pious person breaks in with "Christ is the Answer!" And suddenly all discussion is at an end. Yes, Christ *is* the Answer. But not like that! He is the answer only when the questions are real and have been thoroughly aired and faced.

Bad language is language designed to heighten and exaggerate the differences between men, instead of finding and surveying the common ground of agreement. Bad language is speaking for effect, not to illumine truth but to put the spotlight on oneself. Bad language is talking to win an argument rather than to win a person for his own integrity. Bad language is saying more than we mean and more than we feel, but it is also saying less than we mean and refusing to say what we feel. You see, there is no end to it! No wonder Jesus had so much to say about the perils of speech.

But there is a positive aspect to all this. It is expressed in a picturesque text in Ecclesiastes, and I use it because it is a picture. Macneile Dixon said in his famous Gifford Lectures, "The mind of man is more like a picture gallery than a debating chamber." Here's the picture then. Ecclesiastes, describing a wise man, says, "The sayings of the wise are like goads, and like nails firmly fixed."

Real and profitable conversation, like a goad, prods men on. Like the sheepherder's staff, it urges people on to try new pastures. Would you say that your words do that? How many conversations have you had recently that opened up new horizons? So much of our familiar talk leaves people exactly where we found them, in the old ruts of inherited prejudice and stale convention.

A woman I knew in London was eloquent, witty, and so charming a speaker that she was in great demand at public meetings. But the most eloquent speech I ever heard her give was in her own drawing room to a student listener, a young Indian boy, who looked so forlorn that she went up to make conversation with him. "What are you studying?" she asked brightly. A little taken aback when she discovered he had come to London to study bakery and confectionery, she quickly recovered and said, "And I suppose when you go back to India you will put your studies to use, to improve the standard of living and dietetics?" The boy said nothing. But months later she learned that her words had completely upset his life. He had come to further his own fortunes, and his hostess had taken it for granted that, as a fellow-Christian, he would have nobler ambitions than that, and that he would want to share his training and advantages with his people. Nobody was more surprised than my friend; she was just making conversation. But when a genuine Christian makes conversation, it opens life up in a new way.

Ecclesiastes goes on to say that the words of the wise are not only like goads, but they are also like nails firmly hammered in. We all know the expression "nailing a man down." Sometimes this is the best and finest thing we can do for any man—to nail him down to the truth of what he says. Not to dispute and disagree with him, but to hold him to it, to ask, "Do you really mean that, and are you prepared to follow it to its logical conclusion?"

One way of doing the job of evangelism is to take people seriously on their own terms, to challenge them to stand by the truth of what they profess. In many cases it will be found that they are simply mouthing clichés that they have never examined, and repeating catch phrases and newspaper headlines that in no way represent their deepest working convictions. Many people are better than the things they say, and they live upon unexamined assumptions that contradict their stated creeds.

But nails have another function: they hold things together. As one gets older, one cherishes more the art of constructive conversation. And is not this Christ's final test for a good word, that it cements relations, that it has within it reconciling and healing power? Careless talk is critical without being constructive. Or else, it is merely shocking. But the best thing we can do for another person is not to shock him but to enlighten him. And this is particularly true of our conversation with younger people. Careless talk in front of children, who have, after all, very little experience on which to base a judgment or to sift the chaff from the wheat, is little short of criminal. When, in our grown-up way, we share with them only our sophistication and cynicism, we should not marvel that they grow up cynical and suspicious. We owe our children one thing—their childhood. If we subject them to careless talk, we take the bloom off their childhood and are in danger of turning them into little monsters who know the price of everything and the value of nothing, who become flippant about serious things and irreverent about sacred things. No wonder the most serious warning of Jesus concerned our treatment, verbal and practical, of the young. "Whoever causes one of these little ones who believe in me to sin, it would be better for him to have a great millstone fastened round his neck and to be drowned in the depth of the sea."

the roving eye

*The eye is the lamp of the body. So, if
your eye is sound, your whole body will
be full of light; but, if your eye is not
sound, your whole body will be full of
darkness.*

—MATTHEW 6:22

That great artist and poet, William Blake, once
pointed out that we do not see *with* the eye, but *through*
it. The eye is merely the instrument by which we focus
and illumine the material presented to us. But it is the
man behind the eye who sees. Jesus called the eye the
"lamp of the body." We might think of it as the camera
a photographer uses. What he selects and highlights is
determined by the kind of man he is—artist or pornog-
rapher, man of taste or vulgar snooper. The eye only
records; it is the whole personality that sees.

This is not to say that the eye, being an instrument, is not important; it is. The fact that in common speech we talk about a roving eye, a blind eye, the green eye of the little yellow god, shows that we are aware of the perils of an undisciplined eye. To quote Blake again, "If the doors of perception were cleansed, we should see everything as it is, infinite." We realize that it is our duty and privilege to keep the windows of the soul clean. And the New Testament confirms and underlines our conviction. In fact, it has so much to say on this question that it is difficult to know where to begin.

Let us begin by considering one of the sayings of Jesus about the importance and peril of seeing, one which, for the average man, is the most difficult of all: his judgment about the lustful eye. It is difficult because the man in the street considers it most unfair that he should be condemned for doing something he cannot help doing, that is outside his control. Certainly he would agree that the act of adultery is wrong, but when he reads the saying of Jesus—"But I say to you that every one who looks at a woman lustfully has already committed adultery with her in his heart"—he protests that that is really going too far! He is willing to accept responsibility for what he does, but he can hardly be called to account for what he sees or for those thoughts aroused in him unbidden. Today the eye is simply deluged with lust-provoking material—the shameless way some women dress, the flaunting of sex in advertisements and films and papers. Why, a man would have to be a plaster saint to remain unstirred by it all!

About that two things can be said, one negative, one positive. First on the negative side. A man really is not compelled to look at everything. There is such a thing as a deliberate rationing of the intake of the eye. Simply because there is so much to see and we are bombarded through the eye-gate by cynical and ruthless people, it is up to us to practice a kind of aristocracy of looking. We may have a television set in the house, but we don't have to keep it on all day. Indeed, its very accessibility, its ubiquity, forces upon us a demand for discrimination and choice. Anyone who allows the box to dominate his life should have his head examined.

And on the wider scene, when billboards and shop windows flaunt their wares at us, we are not forced to stand and stare. We can hurry past. Temptation begins where the eye lingers lasciviously, tarries and gloats instead of passing by. I may not be responsible for what I see, but I am responsible for the degree of attention I decide to give to it.

But there is a positive side to this business of seeing. The opposite of a lustful eye is not a blind eye; it is a loving eye! We have almost forgotten today what a loving eye means. Things have come to such a pass that beauty is almost a dirty word. There is no such thing as female beauty any more; there is only sex appeal. So there is a demand laid upon us to cultivate a loving eye, an eye that freely rejoices in the beauty of a face, in the grace of movement and form, without desiring to possess it. I pity the man whose heart does not skip a beat when he sees "the face that launched a thousand ships" or is not moved to admiration by perfect symmetry and coloring. There's something wrong with him! But there's a big difference between rejoicing in beauty and thanking God that it exists, and exploiting beauty to experience a cheap thrill and to inflame the passions.

When Pierre Emmanuel, the French poet, was a boy, he was brought up by a couple of maiden aunts whose training caused him to suffer torments throughout his adolescence. They taught him to distrust and fear beauty. "So," he says, "as a young man I could look at nothing without soiling it." When he finally found deliverance, it was not with the aid of more discipline, more repression, or by averting his face, but by discovering a new attitude to life—a new attitude to God's creation, one of frank, glad appreciation of everything by which God had graced the world and enriched the senses. He began to look at things and see how rare and fine and glorious they were in themselves without any itch to possess and exploit them for personal ends.

As far as seeing the world with a loving eye, we have not even begun! I turn to the magnificent *Letters* of Vincent van Gogh and am amazed at my blindness. Van Gogh looked at everything with eyes washed with wonder and made penetrating by love. Compared with such a man, I am as blind as a bat. How little I know of the world in which I live! The palpitating earth, the tensed muscles of a blade of grass, the texture of skin, the honorable scars of age, the intricate lacery of trees! Nor will I ever see them until my eye is cleansed of lust.

Just as there is a lustful eye, so there is an evil eye. When we talk about the evil eye, we summon up an image of sorcery and black magic. What Jesus meant by an evil eye is an eye that cannot see straight because it is distorted by jealousy and resentment. We recall his words about the laborers in the vineyard. According to the parable, each man received a full day's wages. That was royal generosity. But it immediately provoked antagonism. Those who had done a full day's work got a full day's wages—as agreed upon. But when they saw others who had worked half-time, quarter-time even, they held a protest meeting. Note that they didn't complain about injustice; they complained about generosity. It was this that provoked Jesus' statement about the evil eye. "Is your eye evil because I am good?" he asked. And the answer is yes, our eye is evil. Many of us, instead of rejoicing in our own good fortune, are guilty of contrasting it with the better fortune of others. Worse still, we cannot believe that we are fortunate unless there are others who are receiving less than we are. We cannot feel superior unless there are others who are inferior. What insecurity and evil this reveals. Surely if our inner resources were rich and satisfying and could get along on very little, it would not disturb and agitate us if others were receiving as much and doing less with it! But it does disturb us, alas.

As the opposite of a lustful eye is a loving eye, and the opposite of an evil eye is a generous eye, so the opposite of a death-dealing eye is a life-enkindling eye. We know the expression, "If looks could kill." But they can—and do. A sour look can cast a blight over a whole day. A hateful look can shrivel up a personality. A cold, fishy eye can freeze the marrow of the blood. "Take a pair of sparkling eyes," as W. S. Gilbert says, and what cheer and sunshine they bring into life! And it is not a matter of physical endowment. Eyes can sparkle because there is life behind them; because they are interested eyes, curious about other things than themselves. Even the palest, washed-out eyes can light up in a friendly welcome or glow with sympathy. Some of us are not natural sparklers; we may be dully and stolidly built; but we can and should become aware of this and make a deliberate effort to train our bodies to express the love and interest they feel. Our bodies are the vehicle of our spirit; they are the chief means we have of communicating with others. We should see to it that they communicate efficiently.

Recently I came across this sentence: "They stand in their own light and wonder why it is dark." I shut the book, I read no more. This is the fundamental reason for our lack of good sight. We interpose ourselves between the object and the lamp. We look out upon the world and complain that we have no friends, that we are neglected and overlooked, when the plain truth is that we are standing in our own light, so preoccupied with ourselves that the beams of friendship cannot reach us. It is a truism to say that he who has friends is a friend. But it is a truism more honored in the breach than in the observance. John Oman, the Scots theologian, used to say that people who complain that the atmosphere of a church is chilly tend to forget that "everything within five miles of an iceberg is bound to be cold!" A man finds himself reflected everywhere. If he is mean-spirited, he will see meanness wherever he looks. If he is generous, generosity abounds. Jesus said, "Not what goes into the mouth defiles a man, but what comes out of the mouth, this defiles a man. . . . What comes out of the mouth proceeds from the heart, and this defiles a man. For out of the heart come evil thoughts"—and an evil eye. Long before Freud and company, with their insights into projection and overcompensation, Jesus was warning men that a hypercritical eye is a bad eye. He put it gently in a kind of joke, so that it shouldn't hurt too much—the joke about the fellow who was diligent to pick out the small specks of dirt in the eyes of others, and never noticed that there was a plank sticking out of his own eye. He warned men that "with the judgment you pronounce, you will be judged," for the faults we see in others are usually our own.

"If your eye is sound," said Jesus, "your whole body will be full of light." But the source of light is not the eye. We talk loosely about "inner light," and some sects have built their whole religious philosophy and practice around it, even to the extent of ignoring and despising the light of outer revelation and the light that comes from the Bible and Christian tradition. "Therefore be careful lest the light in you be darkness." A man's only guarantee is to stand where the "light of the knowledge of the glory of God" shines in its full splendor. Browning in his early days said, "Truth is within ourselves, and to know rather consists in opening out a way whence the imprisoned splendor may escape." But in his splendid maturity he realized that there are other things than splendor imprisoned within the human personality. The liberating light comes from beyond and is independent of our moods and achievements. So he sings,

> I stood at Naples once, a night so dark
> I could have scarce conjectured there was earth
> Anywhere, sky or sea or world at all.
> But the night's black was burst through by a
> blaze . . .
> There lay the city thick and plain with spires,
> And like a ghost dishrouded, white the sea.
>> So may the truth be flashed out by one blow
>> And Guido see, one instant, and be saved.

The lamp of our body, even at its best, sheds a dim light on the mystery of things, compared with that light that flashed for a moment upon the landscape in the life of Jesus of Nazareth. On the time scale of the universe it was but a lightning flash, but the darkness was pierced, reality was revealed; and the man who has seen it can never be the same again.

unplanned
budgets

Why do you spend your money for that which is not bread, and your labor for that which does not satisfy?

—ISAIAH 55:2

Have you ever noticed what a large place money, the use of money, one's attitude to money occupy in the New Testament? How often in the parables of Jesus a good businessman is held up as a model! If, he seems to suggest, we devoted the same care and planning to living as we do to making a living, we would not be guilty of the stupid waste and the careless handling we give to the promotion of our own characters. Remember what he said about "what does it profit a man?" The aim of living, as of making a living, is to make a profit, to invest our capital wisely, and to waste nothing.

Yet many people who scrupulously avoid the wrong use of material possessions are guilty of the wrong use of the self. And by wrong I do not mean sinful; I mean just plain silly. I don't mean immoral; I mean foolish. I have been impressed on reading the New Testament lately by the comparative absence on the lips of Jesus of such words as "good" and "bad," "sinful" and "evil." The characters he holds up for inspection are wise men and foolish men, responsible stewards and irresponsible stewards, smart businessmen and stupid businessmen, efficient builders and inefficient builders. Sometimes in our judgment of men we make too much use of purely moral categories and do not stress sufficiently the element of plain common sense.

I recall Dwight L. Moody's handling of the man who came to him in deep trouble—personal, financial, and domestic. He asked the evangelist with a whine of self-pity, "Mr. Moody, what would you do if you were in my place?" And Moody, who was a very down-to-earth character answered, "Man, I wouldn't have gotten in your place in the first place!" Unsympathetic? Yes, but realistic too. We have brought many of our troubles upon ourselves by want of thought, by stupid decisions that were not decisions at all, but spur-of-the-moment impulses.

Among the little foxes that spoil the vines there are

few so destructive and harmful as our unplanned use of our resources.

One wasteful use of life is to expend energy out of all proportion to the result. I believe there is a word for this in physics; I know there is in psychology, and it is "foolishness." Sometimes it is rather attractive and amusing foolishness when it is displayed by naïve and simple people. On my way home from the theater in Edinburgh I used to have to pass through a slum—since torn down. One night I came out of the theater after seeing one of the dullest performances I had ever witnessed; the male cast was insipid, and the females were vapid. But under a street lamp I saw two housewives engaged in earnest, animated conversation. What actresses! What gestures! What rolling eyes and impassioned movements! They surely could not have been discussing anything less momentous than the fate of the United Nations. Actually, I discovered by a little judicious eavesdropping, they were talking about "her" —the woman next door! If they could have diverted a tithe of that soul force into larger channels! But, then, people who lead empty lives have to dramatize themselves in one way or another. That is the only thing that makes life tolerable. And this is true not only of slum housewives, but of suburban matrons. In the suburbs, too, people have been known to make mountains out of molehills just to add a little excitement to the stale round of daily life.

People who employ emotion out of all proportion to the work to be done not only exhaust themselves, but they render themselves ineffective as parents and partners. Some parents do not know when to hold their fire. They shoot full blast at everything, big and small. A minor breach of decorum receives the same indignant treatment as a major crime. They expend the same amount of righteous indignation over a haircut as they do over a traffic ticket or a bit of brutal insensitivity. So when some determined judgment is called for, it does not register; it has all been heard before at precisely the same level of sound and fury. William James put it more tersely when he wrote, "Most people take too intensely the trivial moments of life." They have strong feelings about weak subjects and weak feelings about strong subjects.

Do you remember what Jesus called that? He called it "being Gentile"! And you may be sure he did not mean that as a compliment. "For the Gentiles seek all these things," he said, meaning that they worry themselves sick about what the birds of the air and the lilies of the field take in their stride.

That leads me to the second observation. For what is a "Gentile"? From the point of view of a Jew a Gentile is a man who is lawless, not only literally without the Law, the Torah, but one who has not the sense to see that law is a gift of God, that law is for liberty. This is the great difference between a Gentile and a Jew.

I am not, of course, talking about blood and race now, but about two types of mind—one type which exclaims with the psalmist, "Oh, how I love thy law!" and regards it as the highest wisdom to cooperate with the law; and the other type which regards law as the enemy of liberty and finds its life in resisting it. In any congregation, no matter what its national, ethnic admixture—German, Latin, Polish, or what have you—there is a more fundamental dualism. There is a "Gentile" in us all that regards law as a hampering restriction, and a "Jew" who greets the law with joy because law sets him free to get on with the business of real living.

Many young people think that the highest business of life is to rebel. They love to quote Emerson's stirring words, "Whoso would be a man must be a nonconformist." If they know any more Emerson, it is probably his clarion call, "Hitch your wagon to a star." I recall how that sentence thrilled me when I was younger. Naturally, being a rebel, I thought it meant, "Aim high. Get above the common ruck. Be different!" It has taken me many years to realize that Emerson was counseling not idealism, but realism. He was not exhorting us to essay the impossible, but calling us to harness ourselves to the forces of the universe. All energy is linked to the stars; nothing we achieve here on earth is done without calling upon the resources of the entire cosmos. We do not move a step without utilizing gravity; we do not cast a glance without availing ourselves of light. Emerson was saying something more important than "Aim high." He was saying, in effect, cooperate with life; link yourself to its vast resources; do not squander energy in resisting it.

C. S. Lewis once said in a lecture at Trinity College, Dublin, "Man is the only amateur; all the others are professionals." The world of the animal may be a smaller world than ours, but he is wise enough to use every scrap of it to advantage. We humans, on the other hand, are so wasteful. We squander energy in worry, indecision, self-pity, and depression—things that are rare in the animal kingdom. We expend vital force in fighting ourselves, for what is depression but hostility directed against the self?

Crusty old Thomas Carlyle poked fun at Margaret Fuller for saying, "I accept the universe." "Gad, she'd better!" was his rejoinder, as if there were no alternative. But indeed there is; there is the very common alternative of rejecting it, of spending life resisting, refusing, and restricting, in making gestures of negation and refusal. The world is here for our love and enjoyment, for our use and profit, for our appreciation and delight; yet we frequently turn our backs upon it.

Isaiah asked in astonishment many centuries ago, "Why do you spend your money for that which is not bread, and your labor for that which does not satisfy?" As Henry David Thoreau pointed out so eloquently, when we spend our money, we do not simply spend that—we spend life. "The cost of a thing is the amount of life it requires to be exchanged for it, immediately or in the long run." Because things and possessions, articles of furniture or apparel, are ticketed with tags bearing dollars and cents, we blind ourselves to the fact that the equivalent of those money marks is life effort, is expenditure of vital force, is so many hours and minutes of our all-too-short existence here on earth.

Bertrand Russell, a thinker not usually friendly to Christianity, said, "If men were actuated by self-interest, which they are not, except in the case of a few saints, the world would be paradise." He rightly sees that self-interest is not the same as selfishness; it is thought and work in the proper care and production of the self. To pay proper respect to the self is to aim only at that which satisfies without satiating; it is to pay out one's money (life) only for that which nourishes and builds personality and so makes it useful to God.

In planning a human budget, as in preparing a financial budget, it is wise to beware of the little foxes, those small and apparently trivial eaters-of-life that sap vital energy for no return. A wise spender will ask: What nourishes life? What gives deep and abiding satisfaction? It is to ask what Jesus meant when, resting at Jacob's well, he said, "I have food to eat of which you do not know." To his puzzled disciples Jesus said, "My food is to do the will of him who sent me, and to accomplish his work." The choice of a life's work is perhaps the most fateful choice we make; a job can either enlarge or diminish us. It is to ask what "satisfies" the fundamental needs of a genuine human being, and so to distinguish between striving for reputation and achieving character, between lust and love. Lust, as Shakespeare said, is "the expense of spirit in a waste of shame"; it squanders the energies of life; whereas love, demanding the same expenditure of vitality, gives back that vitality in double measure. It quickens, not deadens, personality. Real goals and healthy effort enhance life, even when they call for hard work. It is said of Rembrandt that he was once admonished by his solicitous apprentices for working too hard on his magnificent canvas, "The Anatomy Lesson." "Master," they said, "you are looking drawn and tired. You are exhausted." "Exhausted!" cried Rembrandt. "No! Spent, yes, but not exhausted. Exhausted means drained, empty, unfulfilled. Spent means fulfilled, completed, inwardly enriched, and happy!" And he could say that because creative effort, when it engages the whole personality and is directed to a great end, does not impoverish life; it enhances it.

acrophobia

They are afraid also of what is high.

—ECCLESIASTES 12:5

The technical term for fear of heights is acrophobia. It is a very common affliction—the dread of climbing ladders, of mountaineering, of flying in airplanes. There are other phobias too. I once knew a husky football player who was terrified of being alone in open spaces. He'd tremble like a guilty thing surprised if he had to walk across an empty lot. That's called agoraphobia. Then there is claustrophobia—the fear of being shut in. That is what keeps some people away from church! And there's hydrophobia the fear of water. But the commonest of all these afflictions is undoubtedly the fear of heights.

Acrophobia is not merely physical however. There is

fear of scaling spiritual and intellectual heights, a dread of being outstanding and conspicuously first-class, a fear of excellence. It reveals itself in the sneering way many people refer to highbrows and eggheads. Some folk make a cult of mediocrity; they just want to be average guys. Of the two mysterious entities called the highest common factor and the lowest common denominator, they prefer to realize the second. They have come to the conclusion that the happiest people in the world are those with average tastes, average attainments, average ambitions. So they choose to live with their feet on the ground.

Behind their choice lie several factors; one of them is the dread of loneliness. I once knew a brilliant young man in Scotland who earned his living in the shipyard, although he had unusual capacities for painting and verbal self-expression. "Sometimes I just hate myself for having ideas and interests that set me apart from my workmates. I both despise them and envy them. In their company I feel so isolated and "different" that I would gladly throw away all my books and canvases and ideas simply to feel 'one of the boys,' a part of that easy, comfortable fraternity whose talk rarely reaches above paypackets and wenching and a good booze-up on Saturday nights."

I find that it is a very real problem for many people besides George. It's a lonely business to be out of step with the crowd. The Latin word for *stranger* is *hostes,* an enemy. There is often a concealed hostility toward anyone who is different, so it is much easier to pretend to go along, to repeat the slogans and clichés of the average man, and to suppress the urge to climb.

There is another reason for the fear of that which is high. Suppose we don't make it? "Humpty Dumpty sat on a wall; Humpty Dumpty had a great fall." If only he had stayed on the ground, there would not have been such a mess! Many a person is held back from attempting excellence through fear of failure. A great artist of the ballet (and ballet consists largely of straining upward and pirouetting on tiptoe!) has analyzed failure into five categories. She says a person may fail because he has chosen the wrong work; he may fail because he has no discipline either in his work or in his emotional life; he may fail because he wishes to fail; he may fail because of grief or sickness or some circumstance beyond his control. But there is an honorable cause of failure: a man may fail because he is trying new and untested ways of expression. "A creative life is bound to have moments of failure simply because it is creative." The artist, in order to stay alive and to be effective, has to keep on experimenting and breaking new ground, even at the cost of failure. And what is true of the artist is also true of all men who wish to be human beings and not robots. It is true in the home, in the church, and in private life. If we are afraid of that which is high, we shall end by giving a good imitation of ourselves; and of all forms of plagiarism, self-plagiarism is the worst. There is a sentence in Psalm 55 that chimes in here. "God will give ear, and humble them . . . because they do not change, and do not fear God." When men settle into the safe, tame routines of religion, they become so self-satisfied, so self-contented, that even God cannot get at them! It is they who open life to new ideas, new achievements, new conquests, and new challenges, who experience most fully the presence of the spirit of that God who is ever bringing new things to pass.

But, to be downright pedestrian, there is a third reason why people fear heights—plain laziness. They would like to experience the rarified air of the mountains, but they have no stomach for the climb. Not for them the "*practice* of the presence of God"; they want it delivered on a plate that, unlike Brother Lawrence, they have not first scrubbed in the kitchen. These are the people for whom prayer is the familiar repetition of a formula which, as they piously and smugly say, they "learned at my mother's knee," although the mathematics they learned at their mother's knee would ill serve them in business and finance. They know nothing, and propose to do nothing, about going to school with the great masters of the spiritual life, like St. John of the Cross or Saint Theresa.

I wish I knew enough Greek to coin the correct term for the opposite of acrophobia. I do not know what to call it, but I know there is such a thing. If some people are afraid of what is high, others are afraid of what is low. They are like Naaman the leper who sought healing at the hands of the prophet of Israel and expected some dramatic, if not traumatic, event. He was incensed when he heard Elisha bid him "go and wash in the Jordan." It was only the common sense of his servants that brought him to a better mind. They said to their indignant commander-in-chief, "If the prophet had commanded you to do some great thing, would you not have done it? How much rather, then, when he says to you, 'Wash and be clean?' "

Many of us want the cure to be as dramatic as the disease, but it seldom is! To break a leg by falling from a scaffold or by leaping into the air after a ball may be dramatic, but healing a broken leg is a very tedious process. And so is the recovery from the sins of the spirit and the excesses of the flesh, as the prodigal son must have discovered when he returned home. After the first excitement of the music and dancing and feasting that greeted his arrival, there were long days when he simply had to slog it out and give the fevers of the past time to subside and depart from his body.

The fear of that which is low prevents many a man casting in his lot with others in the crusade for human betterment. "Politics is a dirty business," he says; and while other men do the dirty work of the world, he hugs his clean, shiny, high ideals to himself.

This mentality operates frequently on the level of religion. I used to know a man who was strongly and intellectually attracted to Christianity; he had read about it and thought about it for years; he possessed a fine library in which volumes by Tillich, Barth, Bultmann, and Bonhoeffer were proudly conspicuous. When I was brash enough to ask him which church he attended, he said, "Church? I don't attend any church. The churches are full of hypocrites." I was tempted to make the time-honored reply, "Well, come in, there is always room for one more!" But I refrained because he was not a hypocrite in the vulgar sense; he was a man with high and noble ideas and ideals, so high that he shrank from putting them into practice. They might get sullied there, down in the rough-and-tumble of ordinary congregational life. He had every sympathy with religion, he told me; what he did not like was organized religion. Is that very different from saying, "I believe in health, but not in organized medicine," or "I subscribe to the idea of education, but I will have no truck with schools"?

In any case, it is the essence of religion to get itself embodied. When John said, "The Word became flesh," he was asserting the principle that religion is not an idea, a sentiment, a holy glow. Religion is the Word in the work, the Word in the world. If a man's spirituality is so refined that it cannot get out of his head into his hands and feet, there is something wrong with it.

One can hardly call George Bernard Shaw an orthodox theologian, but he was very close to the heart of things when he said, "Beware of the man whose God is in heaven." He was rebuking those people who are so spiritual that they are forever in the clouds; so full of bloodless ideals that to engage in such mundane matters as printing Bibles, teaching Sunday school, raising money—in short, giving religion some material embodiment—would be an affront to their pride.

There is a term we often apply to Communism. We call it "godless materialism." Perhaps there is a crime worse than godless materialism, namely godly immaterialism. Surely the true opposite to godless materialism is not immaterialism, but godly materialism, or the reverent, responsible, Christlike handling of what God has handed to us for our use and his glory. As Eric Mascall has so wisely pointed out amid the furor of theological debate today, "What we need is not a secular theology, but a theology of the secular." We must not capitulate to the world, but we dare not despise it either; we must claim it for him to whom it belongs and not disdain the lowly and humble tasks that this will involve.

I had a letter recently from a theologian in England talking about a mutual friend who had just resigned his pastoral charge to enter the academic world. "His tragedy is that he will not shoulder the burden of the commonplace." That's it! And our friend is representative of many. They are scared of that which is low. Of one who reached the heights of all time, it was said, "Though he was rich, yet for your sake he became poor, so that by his poverty you might become rich." It was by bearing the burden of the commonplace—a home where he was misunderstood, a company of disciples who were very ordinary mortals, the day-to-day problems of publicans and sinners—that he prepared himself to bear the burden of the Cross, through which at last he will "draw all men unto himself." And in this regard, the disciple is not greater than his Lord.

ingratitude

Were there not ten cleansed? Where are the nine? Was no one found to return and give praise to God except this for-eigner?

—LUKE 17:17

I think the three most important words in the religious vocabulary are "giving," "forgiving," and "thanksgiving," and the greatest of these is thanksgiving. From thanksgiving all else proceeds. Why is it, then, that we are so reluctant to give thanks?

Let's examine a case history. Here were ten men, suffering from a loathsome disease, the flesh rotting on their bones, so repulsive that they were social outcasts, so dangerous to touch that men shrank even from their shadow. Today, thanks to a chance encounter with a stranger, they were back in circulation, shaking hands with their neighbors, hugging their children, restored to the mainstream of life, accepted by all as normal and natural. It was grand! And how grateful they must have been to their deliverer. But nine of them had slipped off without even bothering to say "thank you." No wonder Jesus was surprised. "Where are the nine?" he asked.

Well, where were they? Let's take an imaginative journey in search of them; let us put them in the witness box to explain their strange behavior. In so doing, we might shed some light on our own strange behavior, for according to biblical arithmetic, nine out of ten of us are guilty of equally inexplicable behavior.

Let's interrogate the first man. Here he comes, beaming all over his face. "Man," he cries, "it's wonderful to be normal again. It was a wonderful moment when I looked down at my poor hands and feet and saw that they were firm and sound and when the man next door looked at me without loathing."

"Then why, oh why, didn't you go back to express your gratitude to the man who had done all this for you?"

"Oh! Did he expect me to? I thought it was his job to do that kind of thing. That's his profession, isn't it— healing people? It never occurred to me that he would expect thanks for doing his duty!"

This fellow has brothers all over the place: people who take for granted all the service and care and kindness that come their way, who never stop to consider that even professional men—doctors, teachers, ministers—are human too, and not just machines functioning with automatic precision. It is only the tenth man who takes time out to thank his old high-school teacher for opening the gates of new life to him; who bothers to drop a note to his doctor after an operation; who thinks of articulating his appreciation to those who serve him faithfully every day.

Among these tenth men was a famous spellbinding preacher in London, F. B. Meyer of Westminster Bridge. He was so popular a speaker that he must have spent a considerable part of his life in trains. But he never got back to one of the great mainline stations, Kings Cross or Paddington, without seeking out the locomotive engineer and saying, "Thank you friend for a safe journey." He never preached more eloquent sermons than that!

But here comes the second man. "You look very fit. Why didn't you go back to thank your benefactor?"

"Well, the fact is, I am not much good at making pretty speeches. You know me; I'm the quiet, reserved type. I thought he would understand without my saying anything about it. I am no hand at expressing myself." Yet this is the very man who, when he was riled and thwarted, could command a beautiful flow of language! Like many another, he could not make pretty speeches, but he was an expert at ugly speeches. Many people who find it hard to twist their tongues round a compliment are eloquent when it comes to complaining and criticizing and faultfinding.

I recall an induction of a new minister in a church in northern England. Northerners pride themselves on being plain, blunt men. One of the deacons at the service of recognition said, "If we like you, we'll say naught, but if we don't we shall tell you!" What a bleak, graceless world it would be if that were the universal practice.

But here's No. 3, a glum, surly-looking chap. We shan't get much out of him, but we can try. "And why didn't you go back to voice your thanks?" "Well, I wasn't sure that it was he. I know that it was he who touched me, and that shortly afterwards my body began to heal up. But that may have been a pure coincidence."

It really is not much use talking to this fellow. He would rather subscribe to all sorts of fantastic things like coincidence, luck, chance, than humble his pride to admit to what stares him in the face. It's a queer mentality, but it is not as rare as it ought to be.

Let's summon No. 4. "Here," says he, "you're asking a lot of questions today. Let me ask you one for a change. This person who healed us—he likes doing that sort of thing, doesn't he? I mean, he gets a lot of satisfaction out of it. Why should he expect thanks for doing what he likes doing?"

There is a certain type of mind which thinks that the only actions worthy of thanks are the disagreeable ones. "Oh, mom likes pottering about the house, cooking, making beds, sewing on buttons, and all that kind of thing. It's her great joy!" Perhaps if mom made a fuss about it and grumbled every time she had a shirt to patch instead of looking as if she enjoyed it, her children would make an effort to say "thanks"! Why do they so often withhold appreciation from the very people who serve them most gladly?

But here is No. 5, in a great hurry, as ever. "Wait a minute, what do you have to say for yourself?" "Oh golly, I meant to go back, honestly I did; but with the excitement of getting home and being reunited with the wife and kids, and finding a hundred and one jobs around the house that had been neglected while I had been away, the question of thanks simply got pushed out."

He reminds me of a young man I used to see in the local hospital. He had been lying there for months, the victim of a motorcycle crash. I would look in on him occasionally because nobody else seemed to. "You wait till I get out of this place," he said. "Everything is going to be different. No more horsing around. I've learned a lot since I have been lying here. The first Sunday I am on my feet, you'll find me round at your church." Well, I'm still waiting! But I know how it is. The boy was quite sincere at the moment of speaking; it's only that since he got out of hospital he has been so busy. It's a condition that many of us suffer from.

But here comes No. 6. "What's your excuse?" "Let me be frank with you," says he. "I was afraid. If I had returned to express my appreciation, I might have got into trouble with the authorities. After all, this man Jesus was not a licensed practitioner, was he? He was just a quack with no standing, no medical certificate, no theological degree, or anything. The scribes and the Pharisees didn't approve of him. It seemed to me that the wisest course was to accept what he had to give and keep quiet about it. After all, there is no sense in sticking your neck out!"

"I'm not ashamed to own my Lord," says the old hymn, "nor to defend his cause." But many of us are, especially if it means running counter to public opinion. How often have we stood by, hearing the most unchristian opinions and knowing they were unchristian, but fearing to make a public protest. "Discretion is the better part of valor," especially in these days of witch-hunting and strong political feeling.

"Yes, and I was afraid too," says No. 7, "but my fear was somewhat different. I was afraid that if I went back and acknowledged my indebtedness to this man Jesus, it would put me under an obligation to him. He might expect me to do something in return! It's very difficult to refuse people to whom one is indebted. My motto is 'Never give people the idea that you are obligated to them,' and then you are free to go your own way!"

This was the reason given to me by a woman not long ago. She admitted—or was it boasted—that she kept herself to herself. "The more involved you become with people," she said, "the more trouble you find. I would rather be independent and neither indebted nor committed to anybody." She even imagined that this was a Christian attitude! Like Jean-Paul Sartre, she evidently felt, "Hell? That's other people!"

"I wonder if you have thought of this?" asks No. 8. "I didn't particularly want to be healed, strange as it may seem to you. To you hale-and-hearty types, health seems to be an unquestioned advantage. Leprosy is an ugly disease. It cuts people off from life. But what if I don't want to live? What if I do not welcome the prospect of getting back into the hurly-burly, the rat race, the scramble to make a living? What if I was glad to shuffle off the burden of responsibility? There are compensations even in illness, in a life of permanent invalidism. But now thanks to this Jesus, I am forced back onto the treadmill, with a job to look for and, when I've got it, to hold down."

This is an extreme case. Or is it? I wonder if it is not the commonest case of all. I don't mean physically. I mean that there are many, many spiritual invalids who prefer to be just that. If they were fighting-fit, they might be called upon to fight! If they had abundant life, they might be called upon to share it! How many of us muddle through life, content with our mediocrity because mediocrity absolves us from essaying tasks we do not want to face? E. E. Cummings was never more inspired than when he coined the word "undead." How well it describes the condition many of us are in!

"And No. 9, what have you to say for yourself?" "You didn't think? No wonder you didn't thank." "Think" and "thank" come from the same root. *Denken* and *danken* are intimately related, not merely etymologically, but psychologically and spiritually. "It is a good thing to give thanks to the Lord," cried the psalmist. Great praisers are great livers. To reflect even for a moment on "our creation, preservation, and all the blessings of this life" is to stir up the spirit. To acknowledge our debt to the past is to make ourselves available to the present.

No little fox can get in among the vines if the vineyard is girded with praise. Even when the vineyard was the Garden of Gethsemane, Jesus walled it round with praise.

let George do it!

The sons of the prophets said to Elisha, "See, the place where we dwell under your charge is too small for us. Let us go to the Jordan and each of us get there a log, and let us make a place for us to dwell there." And he answered, "Go."

—II KINGS 6:1-2

I imagine this was one of the proudest moments in Elisha's career, when his "boys" took the initiative and not only proposed a building scheme but accepted responsibility for it. Every man carried his own beam.

I suppose the sons of the prophets were what today would be called university students. They were not literally and biologically prophets' children, but young prophets in training. They were the bright young men of the community. And they were not all theologians or preachers, for in that time and at that place, prophets were not parsons only; they were statesmen, politicians, bureaucrats, educators, organizers, and civil servants. In a community where there was no separation of church and state, everything—from diet to dying, from sanitary regulations to prayer rules, from economics to ecumenicity—was conducted under the auspices of religion. All careers in those days were church careers. Law was the Law of Moses, education was priestly instruction, administration was carrying out the organization laid down in the sacred Scriptures.

So these sons of the prophets were what we today would call the young intelligentsia. And then, as now, these bright young men were dissatisfied. Who would have them otherwise? "Look here!" they said to Professor Elisha. "The place where we dwell under your charge is too small for us. There isn't room to swing a cat. We want a bigger place, where we can live and work without getting in each other's way, a dwelling with some privacy for study and reflection."

But then they went on to say something that is not so characteristic of today. "What we are asking for, Elisha, is your permission for us to go out and do the job ourselves. Let us go, each man carrying his own log, and let us get on with the job." Apparently there was not a Hamlet among them, no one who cried with the young Prince of Denmark,

> The time is out of joint; O cursed spite,
> That ever I was born to set it right!

Not a single one of them whined, "Let George do it!"

Most people today are aware that the world is in a terrible state, cramped and ramshackle. Morality in America, if we are to believe the muckraking magazines and politicians out of office, is at its lowest ebb. From nonexistent oil wells to cheating at examinations, from dope addiction to vandalism, from price-fixing to labor racketeering—the list is endless. Many decent people hold up their hands in horror and cry, "There ought to be a law!" And they forget that there is a law, a moral law, that is binding upon them as well as upon other people, and that morality, like charity, begins at home. Morality is not living within the law (but only just!); morality is a passion for righteousness, for the spread of right relations. It is not toeing the line, but venturing into new areas of reconciliation and responsibility. It is saying, with the sons of the prophets, "Let us go, each carrying our own log."

What enlarges the world is not multiplying laws; you may multiply laws and multiply crime too! Of course laws are necessary; there has to be a structure within which men may find liberty and opportunity for personal growth. But what prevents the world from sliding downhill is the acceptance of personal, private integrity; the resolute determination of each citizen to add his beam to increase the spaciousness and dignity of the house.

It is one thing to "deplore" racial strife; it is another to make one's personal contribution to easing it. One young "son of the prophets," a recent graduate of our theological seminary, felt the burden and the shame of the racial situation so acutely that he gave up his position as assistant minister of a white suburban church to shepherd an all-Negro congregation in Texas. He inherited there a literally ramshackle building, a tiny and discouraged congregation, and a salary well below the one he was receiving in the white church. He is paying two thousand dollars a year for the privilege of carrying his own beam! And he is also enjoying himself immensely!

Like the weather, which everyone talks about and does nothing about, the educational system of our land is the subject of constant debate and vocal dissatisfaction. Many teachers, cramped by the system, cry, "The place where we dwell is too small for us!" But it takes a free spirit, like Sylvia Townsend-Warner, to use the freedom she has without waiting for "them" to move. It is an inspiration to read her book, *Teacher*, to see what can be done by one woman taking responsibility into her own hands, thinking for herself, devising her own program, and carrying it through against the inertia of the system.

The motto of the Christopher society is "It is better to light a small candle than to curse the darkness." But one does not have to be a Roman Catholic to belong to that society, nor be enrolled on its official list. A certain Negro woman in our vicinity is, I daresay, a Baptist, but she has personally hand-printed over four hundred stickers in her own backyard, with the exhortation: "Be Wise. Stay in School." She recognizes the vital part that education must play in the Negro revolution and that legal rights are nothing—may even be worse than nothing—without higher standards of skill and learning. But unlike many of her race, she is not content to beef about it. The placard she flaunts is a constructive one, and she has made herself personally responsible for seeing that it is displayed.

Every institution in the land is an inverted pyramid— too few responsible and committed people bearing a big mass of inertia, supporting an overweight of spectators and well-wishers. This is unfortunately true of everything from garden clubs to the United Fund, from churches to trade unions. And very often—human nature being what it is—the most vocal critics are the least involved persons. Maybe their criticism is the outcome of a guilty conscience?

From this gloomy survey, let's turn back to Elisha's pupils. We may be sure that as the sons of the prophets got their new headquarters built, they themselves grew to greater stature. Emerson once said, "An institution is the lengthened shadow of one man." But it is equally true to say, "Every great man is the product of an institution that he has helped to foster and build." We may be sure that those young students in Elisha's academy grew in dignity and self-respect. The man who is a mere sponger on life is an inferior being, and he knows it. Sponging has a subtle, downgrading influence upon everything he does. We may guess also that these sons of the prophets not only grew in personal stature, but that they also became better prophets, better professional men. Because they accepted responsibility for the enlargement of their own school, they entered more deeply into its purpose and mission. Donald W. Shriver, Director of Experimental Study of Religion and Society, North Carolina State University, writing in *The Journal,* described a "lethargy that I often encounter among students of engineering on a state university campus. These men are dogged students of their discipline, but a certain weariness attends their study." The same weariness has been observed in other disciplines— medicine, law, education, and even theology—and I sometimes wonder how much of this is because these favored students are recipients of gifts and traditions and resources they had no hand in bringing to being. They are heirs to fine buildings, superb facilities, financial and intellectual endowments that they can point to with pride but can claim no part in making. "Others have labored, and you have entered into their labor."

What is true of the academic world is abundantly true also of the wider world of national life, of culture, of business, and civics. And certainly true in the world of the church. We are all parasites on the past. For instance, the denomination I serve has not erected a single seminary in this vast area; for the supply of our ministers we sponge on Illinois or Missouri! What is worse, we have not opened a single school of higher learning;

we leave that to the Methodists and the Presbyterians. Nor have we erected a single hospital. Thank God for the Baptists! We have the excuse, of course, that compared with those affluent denominations we are a poor lot, but even so, it should hurt our conscience more.

The sons of the prophets were a guild, but each man was also a person; and it is on the personal level that they were such an inspiring example. None of them waited for a law to be passed; each man passed a law for himself! He picked his own log and put his own shoulder under it and hoisted it into place.

So often we expect the other man to make the first move. We complain that the world is a cold place and light no fire of our own. Two people came to me in quick succession the other day. One said, "I think yours is a very cold church." The other said, "I think our church is the warmest church I have ever belonged to." The difference was in the pronouns. "Your church," said one; "our church," said the other. So it is in friendship. People with no friends are hardly friendly. They invite no response because they make no signals. Friendship is not merely a question of going halfway; it is a matter of going all the way—flashing welcome signals with the eyes, putting feelings into gestures of welcome, and, above all, showing a genuine interest in people.

It is the same way with national and civic life. We are hearing much in these days about states' rights and federal rights. To hear some people talk you would think that America would be the Garden of Eden tomorrow if only all rights were vested in the separate states. That is a matter of argument; but what is beyond argument is that there are also personal rights, and personal duties and personal responsibilities—and that these are among the least exercised of all rights. Yet without them a city cannot continue nor a nation flourish.

As World War I was ending, the Manchester journalist C. E. Montague warned his countrymen that reconstruction would not come by "congress, conference or general committee or subcommittee, or any other expedient for talking in company instead of working alone." This is the individual's job, he said. "To get down to work, whoever else idles; to tell no lies, whoever else may thrive on their use . . . to take less from your world than you give it . . ."—these are the qualities upon which a spacious future will be built.